ONE SINCERE MOMENT

ONE SINCERE MOMENT

THE ANSWER

In Search Of Always Right

BILL B MOSS JR.

XULON ELITE

Xulon Press Elite
2301 Lucien Way #415
Maitland, FL 32751
407.339.4217
www.xulonpress.com

Unless otherwise indicated, Scripture quotations taken from the King James Version (KJV) – *public domain*.

Paperback ISBN-13: 978-1-66287-783-4
Ebook ISBN-13: 978-1-66287-784-1

Contents

Preface

THE GOAL OF this book is my desire for you, and your loved ones, to have abundant life here and a home in Heaven someday. Unlike most books, which are read from front to back to tell a story; *One Sincere Moment* is designed to examine individual issues. Choose the issues that are important to you and compare what's written with your personal worldview. If you read it cover-to-cover, you'll notice some repetition because issues overlap over time.

When looking at the various media reports of our day, we see that there are plenty issues and opinions, but there are few meaningful solutions. You'll notice the reports here are from several years. I started recording my thoughts in 2010. Additionally, some issues listed in the Table of Contents are not directly addressed. I've tried to list every issue from A to Z. That said, The God of Heaven has a principle, answer, and solution for them all. I just do not have enough time or lifespan to pen details on every issue. That said, if there is an issue or question you would like to consider, contact me at countdown21@gmail.com. God knows the number of grains of sand on the seashore and that number changes with every wave and every time someone leaves the seashore. Speaking of the miraculous, have you ever searched for the world population clock on the internet? It constantly changes, too. That brings me back to the goal of this book, which will be repeated several times because it is all important. You, your loved ones, and everyone in your sphere of influence are living miracles. At the issuing of this book, there are 8 billion, and counting, people on the planet and only one like you. Again, you are a miracle. God loves you and therefore your life matters. Your life matters to God and your life matters to me. Consider Christ

*ANEW and know *Absolutely Nothing Else Works, apart from trusting in Him, too.

Finally, I would be remiss not to, first, give thanks to the God of Heaven, Christ Jesus, for gloriously saving me on November 21, 1999. I am so thankful for the grace extended to me and to all who will come to Him by faith. I'm also thankful for all the people He has put in my path over the years. My wife of more than forty years has been here for me through the good and bad times. I praise the Lord, He helped us; we have decided of forever. He has also blessed me with great children, grandchildren, and a glorious church family. A special thanks to God for Pastor Tony Jones' preaching *Christ Jesus is The Answer,* which helped me decide on the title of this book. Finally, I thank God for Pastor Dan Patterson preaching *This I Believe,* which confirmed my desire to share ISOAR (In Search Of Always Right) with whosoever will listen.

"I am Alpha and Omega, the beginning and the ending, saith the Lord, which is, and which was, and which is to come, the Almighty" (Revelation 1:8).

God Loves You! He desires a personal relationship with you that is real; He wants to be you Savior and your Friend.

"God so loved the souls of sinners, That He paid a precious price, my soul He loved and treasured, When He died to save my life, When He died to save my life" – *Patch The Pirate.*

Dear Lord,
My prayer is that you be glorified and that the spirit of God takes the things of God and makes them real to all who read this; in Jesus' name. Amen.

Introduction:

One Sincere Moment

IN PSALM 116:11 the psalmist, David, said; "I said in my haste, all men are liars." Well, as of the issuing of this book I have been on the planet more than sixty-three years and have met a lot of people. Additionally, I have looked into many mirrors; And you know, the psalmist was right.

We are so phony and have been for so long that we believe our lies. I've probably overstated the following but, we've been so wrong for so long that right appears wrong. What we need is one sincere moment. We need to take an honest, sincere look at our worldviews and admit that something is amiss. We are full of opinions and void of solutions.

One Sincere Moment gives us an interactive way to analyze our personal worldviews and, at the same time, come up with solutions that are best for all of us. You see, I'm convinced that if we are willing to compare worldviews, we will easily determine what is lacking.

You'll notice the use of many acronyms; this is due to my former government service. I am promoting a detailed system for comparing worldviews called "In Search Of Always Right" (ISOAR). The key to this is B.C. to A.D. That is a play on words. In this context it means: By Comparison (B.C.) we finish well After Death (A.D.).

I'm considering taking ISOAR onto social media platforms, stay tuned. See the "I" section (Chapter 9) for the conditions that will make this endeavor successful. Yes, we all can soar on eagles' wings in this present, troubled, world.

I am confident that the King James Biblical worldview is superior to any other worldview for solutions to our many troubling issues.

Chapter 1

Apostasy: The Beginning of the End

"California parents request judge block public schools from asking students to pray to Aztec gods."[1]

Yes, apostasy is where it all begins. America, we've got issues. In every nation or people group, the path to destruction begins when we turn away from the one true God as depicted in the King James Bible. Our startling moral decline is part of what inspired me to write this book. I was convinced some time ago that we are sliding downhill from a Godly generation. I fear that we have gotten so far away from our godly heritage that we are beyond recovery. That said, I realize that to truly be a genuine Christian nation is defined as having an agreed upon desire to trust in, and follow, the teachings of Christ Jesus. The debate is moot on whether we were ever that nation as we are living in the here and now. Our early leaders did recognize the God who loves us. If you have any doubt about our godly heritage, just visit the monuments and archives in Washington D.C.

Saying you're Christian and being one are two different things though. I hope to clarify this and other misconceptions about Christianity along the way, so keep reading.

"One nation under God," is nonnegotiable, which means we are under the authority of our Creator if we like it or not.

You may agree with me that the United States is the best place to live, but it is impossible to find a single nation on the planet that is completely thriving socially, economically, and politically. Today every nation is in decline. What does your worldview provide that assures a continuous, thriving nation? Now a bit GOoD news (God's Good News): Anything that is good comes from The God of Heaven, Christ Jesus. He is The Light; everything He does, or allows, is always, always, right.

"Every good gift and every perfect gift is from above, and cometh down from the Father of lights, with whom is no variableness, neither shadow or turning" (James 1:17).

Notice, via representative media reports throughout this book, the three steps that lead to a national failure: apostasy, moral awfulness, and political anarchy.

1. Apostasy: "Are the Ten Commandments still relevant today?"[2]
When a nation starts to deny the authority of its Creator or is established denying the existence of the one true God at its inception, the path to destruction begins (Romans 1:18–25). The Ten Commandments are not suggestions. That's what makes them relevant (James 1:25). You see, we can't keep the Ten Commandments (Romans 8:3–4).They show us our need of The Savior (Galatians 3:24).

"The issue with; Keep the Christ in Christmas."[3]

"Christianity is about acceptance?" No, Christianity is about following Christ. His birth is what Christmas is all about. Without Christ all we have is 'mas;' which celebrates nothing of eternal value because we are missing a Savior. Eternity is at stake. Christ Jesus came to save sinners.

"For unto us a child is born, unto us a son is given: and the government shall be upon his shoulder: and his name shall be called

Wonderful, Counsellor, The mighty God, The everlasting Father, The Prince of Peace" (Isaiah 9:6).

2. Moral awfulness: *House of Cards* ending amid Kevin Spacey's sexual harassment claim and Trump declaring an opioid crisis a "public health emergency."[4]
Denial leads to confusion, which is highlighted by lawlessness, violence, and broken lives (Romans 3:12–18).

3. Political Anarchy: "California clears first hurdle to breaking into three states."[5]
"Antifa apocalypse? Anarchist group's plan to overthrow Trump regime."[6]

Thankfully, the United States is not at that final stage yet, but eventually the final "nail-in-the-coffin" is political anarchy. When the general population has non-righteous leadership, with no personal relationship with its Creator, it rebels and destruction follows (Proverbs 29:2).

The good news: In Christ Jesus there is equity. There's no divisiveness because there are no individuals (Galatians 3:26). Everyone is welcomed and anybody can come (John 5:24).
Come as a giver, not a taker; and leave a receiver, changed by The Maker, (Matthew 5:3).
Consider Christ ANEW, nothing else will do (1Timothy 2:5–6).

Again, what does your worldview offer that will unite all Americans?

Finally, I'd be remiss not the mention abortion in this "A" section as everything begins there. Nothing can be more morally wrong than to push for justice and equality while killing the unborn. Pastor, Tony Jones, so rightly said, "If you are wrong about life, you are likely wrong about everything else." The greatest excuse given for abortion is pregnancy attributed to rape and incest. While this is a valid concern, ultimately this falls short of validity also. Again, *One Sincere Moment* reveals that we have a sin problem. We need to train our boys and girls, men and women, what righteous behavior is. Rape, incest, and fornication are wrong. Again, any intimacy outside of the marriage relationship between one man and woman is wrong and should be avoided. Change the heart of the children and you'll change their behavior.

"Train up a child in the way he should go: and when he is old, he will not depart from it" (Proverbs 22:6).

That said, we need to enact compassionate assistance for victims, encouraging them to have the child because we all will stand before God someday and give an account for our decisions. The sacrifices made in this life will be worth it all in that day. Additionally, very harsh punishment needs to be enacted for offenders to send a strong message against wicked behavior. Righteousness and justice that the God of Heaven commands requires it. What about cases where the life of the mother is in jeopardy? The same precedent applies. The intent of the heart needs to support life. Doctors will also have to give an account for their actions. Therefore, the greatest desire should be to save everyone involved. The God of Heaven is pro-choose; that is, He allows you to choose but He controls the consequences. He cannot coexist with imperfection; therefore we must adhere to His Word which is always right.

While living and writing this book, I came to some great truths. The God of Heaven is always at work. Everything He does or allows (good or bad), is for our good, His glory, and ultimately a blessing. Within His great love for us, God has established two great pillars: discovery and sacrifice. Yes, the more we all read the Bible the better. We're seeing the consequences of a world that wants do live apart from the Creator.

Men, like it or not, we have been entrusted with leadership roles in this world. A chapter of Proverbs a day is a good beginning because most months it is literally one chapter a day. That said, out of thanks to God for His instruction book to mankind, we can read more than one chapter every now and then.

"Better is the poor that walketh in his uprightness, than he that is perverse in his ways, though he be rich" (Proverbs 28:6).

"Correct thy son, and he shall give thee rest; yea, he shall give delight unto thy soul" (Proverbs 29:17).

"Every word of God is pure: he is a shield unto them that put their trust in him" (Proverbs 30:5).

"Who can find a virtuous woman? For her price is far above rubies" (Proverbs 31:10).

Consider Christ ANEW, God's Word is never through. "Heaven and earth shall pass away, but my words shall not pass away" (Matthew 24:35).

What we all need is *One Sincere Moment*. God loves you and He desires a personal relationship with you that is real. He wants to be your Savior and your friend.

Chapter 2

Been There Done That, But Now, Because He Lives, Brainwashing

"Pull Your Children Out. Candace Owens Says Public Schools Are Brainwashing Children To Embrace 'Marxist Principles.'" [7]

"Ancient Mars lake could be hiding fossilized signs of alien life." [8]

WE OFTEN HEAR that "religion" brainwashes or indoctrinates individuals into not being independent thinkers. Well, ponder this: I attend my local church on average for 12 hours a week. I sleep approximately fifty-six hours. Therefore, I am being influenced by a sin-cursed, ungodly, world for about 100 hours a week. Now, who is being brainwashed?

"Jane Fonda, 83, shares what she thinks happens when you die... and it's truly uplifting."[9]

"Are We Living in a Post-Happiness World? With happiness harder to come by these days, people are grasping at any moment of joy they can get." [10]

With all due respect to Ms. Fonda, saying our energy lives on or, even encouraging others in the here and now is moot if we all die and end up separated from anything good for all of eternity. This is yet another futile attempt to find satisfaction apart from the God of Heaven, Christ Jesus.

Like a lot of us, I tried just about anything and everything to be happy, but apart from God, in Christ Jesus, it is a futile effort. This is another one of those things we have a hard time being sincere about. What does your worldview provide that offers genuine happiness? Our degree of happiness is ultimately determined by a life lived in agreement or disagreement with the one who died for the enemy, you and me (Romans 5:10).

Obedience to God's Word is the only way to find contentment in this sin-sick world. Some say remembering the past can aid in avoiding mistakes in this life, but it is not where you've been that counts; It is where you're going when you die. You see, we all will keep the most important appointment, which is death.

"And as it is appointed unto men once to die, but after this the judgment" (Hebrews 9:27).

The good news is that God loves you. He desires a personal relationship with you that is real. He wants to be your Savior and your friend.

Chapter 3

Consider Christ During Climate Change and COVID-19

Comparison is the key. Is manmade climate change or COVID-19 as deadly as reported? View the following reports and compare the King James Biblical worldview with yours?

"Pfizer scientist admits that natural antibodies are probably better than vaccination." [11]

"Tragic milestone as COVID-19 deaths eclipse 700,000 in U.S."[12]

"Greta Thunberg roasts world leaders for being 'blah, blah, blah'on climate action." [13]

"EPA plans to roll back Clean Power Plan, major Obama-era climate rule."[14]

Ownership, Stewardship, and a "Climate" of Division
Understanding that there is underlying business, economic, and job-related motivating factors here, this reply will discuss the issue of climate change or global warming. This is yet another divisive issue, and like every issue that divides, the culprit is a lack of fundamental or agreed upon truth. Some experts say we are destroying the planet, others say it's all a hoax. What are we average folks to believe?

Now, the GOoD news (God's Good News): The King James Biblical worldview is one of ownership and stewardship. Anything that I own is God-given. Everything from my person to my possessions is God's (1 Corinthians 6:19–20). Therefore, I am merely a steward of what God has blessed me with. This carries over to the world I live on. The One who created it all (Genesis 1:1) owns it all, and He can sustain it.

We can find common ground and agree that we are to be good stewards of the planet, but this world will not be saved or destroyed by man-made effort alone (Genesis 8:20–22). The sovereign God of the universe will not allow us to destroy this planet as He plans to conquer, and then renew it, someday (1 Corinthians 15:21–26). The eternal plan of God is a new Heaven and earth that never ends (Revelation 21:1–4). Why? Because His plan is centered on His love for us (John 3:16–17).You see, He plans to restore all things to its original, pre-sin, condition: A personal love relationship between God and mankind, the crown of His creation walking with Him in the cool of the day (Revelation 21:5–7).

"Hubble Space Telescope Spots Earliest and Farthest Star Known and Characterizing the earliest galaxies in the universe, only 200 million years after the Big Bang"[15]

Mankind, as smart as we are, has not answered where the energy came from that caused the Big Bang. That said, astronomers have acknowledged that the universe is expanding. You see, when The God of Heaven stretched out the heavens, He never established an ending point.

"Thus saith God the LORD, he that created the heavens, and stretched them out; he that spread forth the earth, and that which cometh out of it; he that giveth breath unto the people upon it, and spirit to them that walk therein" (Isaiah 42:5).

Consider Christ ANEW. He will radically change your worldview.

I am COVID-19 Positive

No, I have been tested and found negative for COVID-19 but, I'm positive that America is being tested. You see, we are a nation reaping the inevitable consequences of life without God. Although, during the pandemic; even with all the concern, care, and cancellations; we were given an opportunity to be still (Psalm 46:10). That is a positive development. The time is now to consider Christ as eternity is at stake.

During the pandemic, the God of Heaven allowed every busy aspect of the American life to be removed. He said, "Be still and know I am God." (Psalm 46:10a). The pandemic is doing what the God of Heaven desires the most: drawing people to Himself (Matthew 11:28–30). His love for us has superseded our rejection of Him and, for some of us, this could be the last chance to repent and believe the Gospel (1 Corinthians 15:3–4).

Former President Trump's call for a national day of prayer is another positive development, but don't be deceived because, The first prayer God responds to from an unbeliever is a prayer of repentance; a desire for salvation (Romans 10:9). The genuine believer has nothing to fear while others fret the pandemic, we enjoy abundant life now and have a home in heaven someday. (Romans 6:22).

"Surgeon General Adams Warns of 'Saddest Week of Most American's Lives as COVID-19 Pandemic Spreads."[16]

Does your worldview see positive and negative consequences of a pandemic?

As we search for an answer for COVID-19; a cure, comfort, or a vaccine; the truth is: While some struggle to simply take a breath, we must deal with the reality of imminent death. The good news is that the meaning of the saddest week, (i.e., Easter) could be for you what it was for Christ Jesus after that first Holy week. I see a victorious *C.O.V.I.D.

acronym: *Christ Offers Victory In Death. The road to Calvary ends in victory for all who believe and put their trust in Him. Ultimately, the choice is yours but remember, we control the choices, not the consequences. Consider Christ *ANEW and Happy Easter, He loves you.*Absolutely Nothing Else Works.

"Come unto me, all ye that labour and are heavy laden, and I will give you rest. Take my yoke upon you, and learn of me; for I am meek and lowly in heart: and ye shall find rest unto your souls. For my yoke is easy, and my burden is light" (Matthew 11:28–30).

"For I delivered unto you first of all that which I also received, how that Christ died for our sins according to the scriptures; And that he was buried, and that he rose again the third day according to the scriptures"(1 Corinthians15:3–4).

"For whosoever shall call upon the name of the Lord shall be saved" (Romans 10:13).

God loves you. He desires a personal relationship with you that is real. He wants to be your Savior and your friend.

Chapter 4

Dancing, Declaration of Dependence, Doubt and the Detached Mind, Death and the Death Penalty, DACA, Double Trouble, Defund the Police, D.O.C.T.R.I.N.E.S.

"Missouri executes Ernest Johnson for 1994 triple murder."[17]

"A Sadistic Monster with No Heart, Texas Man Gets Two Life Sentences for Crashing Propane Tank-Filled Truck into RV with Pregnant Ex Inside."[18]

"What is the maximum age for a human? Scientists make a striking claim."[19]

"Biden Administration Drops 7 Death Penalty Requests."[20]

"DC Mayor bans dancing at weddings; it's insane."[21]

THIS IS YET another case where worldview comes into play. The premise is that dancing falls under COVID-19 restrictions because of the closeness involved. It does appear to be insane because those who get close in public are likely already close privately, and as a talk show host opined, "the bride and groom will probably be consummating the marriage shortly." This same conservative host went on to reveal his ignorance of spiritual things by berating believers who shun carnal dancing. You see, it still comes down to the intent of the heart. Why are people dancing at the wedding or anywhere else?

Now, the GOoD news (God's Good News): Genuine followers of Christ Jesus stay away from most dancing events because of its sinful underlying nature. Does it glorify God? The other reason is the care for others. We would rather abstain from things we know causes others to stumble, as most dancing has a perverse sexual connotation associated with it; Add the alcohol element and sin wins, and those who partake eventually lose. Christians desire to be different to make a difference. Eternity is a long time to be separated from anything good. People need the Lord.

"Whether therefore ye eat, or drink, or whatsoever ye do, do all to the glory of God" (1 Corinthians 10:31).

"Wine is a mocker, strong drink is raging: and whosoever is deceived thereby is not wise" (Proverbs 20:1).

How does your worldview explain death and the death penalty?

Death and judgment are unintended acts of God. When the God of Heaven breathed into man the breath of life He meant for mankind to live an abundant life here on earth in a close and perfect, unending, loving relationship with Him. Therefore, the natural desire for all human beings is to fight to physically live. Meaning, I will naturally struggle to live as I take my final breath here and rejoice the moment I awake in His presence. Yes, sin has consequences.

"For the wages of sin is death; but the gift of God is eternal life through Jesus Christ our LORD" (Romans 6:23).

This is a testament of God's sovereign power; what the original sin or disobedience ruined, He, the Lord Jesus Christ, has provided healing through His life, death, burial, and resurrection. Whoever comes to Him by faith receives abundant life here and eternal life.

"My sheep hear my voice, and I know them, and they follow me: And I give unto them eternal life; and they shall never perish, neither shall any man pluck them out of my hand. My Father, which gave them me, is greater than all; and no man is able to pluck them out of my Father's hand" (John 10:27–29).

"For such an high priest became us, who is holy, harmless, undefiled, separate from sinners, and made higher than the heavens" (Hebrews 7:26).

Justice, God requires it. Jury recommends death in Oklahoma beheading case, Alton Nolen had repeatedly requested to be sentenced to death."[22]

This caught my interest due to its unique circumstances. The alleged murderer wanted the death penalty, but no one granted his request. What does your worldview give as justice for one or even fifty-eight lives taken by an evildoer in Vegas? If this Oklahoma report is true, what's lacking is the basic principle of right, wrong, and justice. Now the GOoD news (God's Good News): God gives life and He determines when and if it is taken. The King James Biblical worldview is one of justice not revenge. God established the death penalty in the beginning and never repealed it (Genesis 9:6). The sovereign God of the universe gave mankind civil authority to protect life by purging evil. The God-given responsibility of any judge or jury is to render justice for victims. You see, if I get away with sin, your good work is in vain.

Unfortunately, the Vegas shooter is already gone, and his eternal fate is sealed (Hebrews 9:27–28). His opportunity to be forgiven is over. God loves murderers even though their intent is to murder, but God loves the victim just as much as the transgressor. Therefore, when we take a life, He requires us forfeiting ours.

It comes down to the intent of the heart. Christ Jesus died for all sin (Romans 6:23). Anyone, even a murderer, who has a change of heart, repents of personal sin, and genuinely trusts Jesus Christ as their personal Lord and Savior will enjoy eternal life where all is good, all the time (John 10:27–30).

The hard truth is that we are all guilty. And death, the penalty for sin, is universal. God's original plan of an abundant, unending, sinless life here on earth, in a loving relationship with Him, was subverted when sin and disobedience entered the universe (Isaiah 14:12–14; Romans 5:12). But the sorrowful sleep of physical death is temporary for the true believer, as joy comes in the morning.

"For to me to live is Christ, and to die is gain" (Philippians 1:21). Consider Christ ANEW. He loves you (1 Corinthians 15:22).

The Detached Mind

Have you ever wondered why dreams are so crazy? Well, during my time in military service we had a saying, "Garbage in garbage out." The service context was that the quality of data input, or lack thereof, determines the quality of the output. This may be the cause of most of our weird dreams. We flood our subconscious with ungodly things and reap the consequences. Notwithstanding, while trauma and stress have also been labeled as culprits, sin is still the underlying issue.

Now the GOoD news (God's Good News): The God of Heaven is not limited to our waking hours. When we surrender all to Him and trust Him as our personal Lord and Savior, we can lay upon our pillows at night with confidence. "Thy word have I hid in mine heart, that I might not sin against thee" (Psalm 119:11). Put away worldly things and fill that space with Godly things. Life, with contentment, is great gain.

Consider Christ ANEW. The rest is easy, too.

"Sienna confronted by immigration activists in bathroom"[23]

"The Deferred Action for Childhood Arrivals, Historic immigration debate to grip Senate." [24]

"Judge rules against Trump administration on rescinding DACA."[25]

Demanding amnesty for illegal immigrants?
This appears to be a difficult issue to address because of the politics involved, but like most issues, we have missed or ignored the root-cause of the problem. What does your worldview give as a solution for the immigration issue?

Now, the GOoD news (God's Good News): While having compassion for those who are oppressed and desiring to escape wicked regimes, the King James Biblical worldview is that there are several complimentary sins at work here: First, the sin of individuals (i.e. the grownups) who would knowingly enter a sovereign nation illegally. The second sin is a nation that would enable this activity by not addressing it immediately (i.e. deferred action). Yes, that is actually a sin problem and now the consequences are becoming evident.

"Righteousness exalteth a nation: but sin is a reproach to any people" (Proverbs 14:34).

The God of Heaven gave us civil authority. We are a nation of laws. By the way, "One Nation Under God" is nonnegotiable. He, Christ Jesus, is the King. Our sin is that we don't have a heart for the King, therefore we aren't good stewards of what He has entrusted to us. The solution is to put a stop to all illegal immigration by eliminating the temptation to enter illegally by building a wall, enhancing border surveillance and address the hiring of illegal immigrants. Streamline the legal immigration process: anyone who wants to assimilate is welcomed; Identify everyone who is illegally here, this can be aided by getting employers involved. Evaluate and determine each individual's fate on a case-by-case basis (background/ security checks etc). Finally, we need to revisit the anchor baby citizenship issue. Should a person here illegally be rewarded for doing anything? Yes, confusion is a consequence of sin. That is why we shouldn't let sin begin and continue to fester.

"So, Christ was once offered to bear the sins of many; and unto them that look for him shall he appear the second time without sin unto salvation" (Hebrews 9:28). Consider Christ ANEW. He offers an incorruptible citizenship for you.

Again, a few steps toward an immigration solution: First is a desire to glorify God by wanting all to be rightly related to God through Christ Jesus. The Gospel needs to be given to everyone. Changing the hearts of men and women will change their behavior and destiny for all of eternity. Again, here are the steps that should take place:

1. Publicly admit that we have sinned and allowed illegal activity to thrive in America. From this date forward, any illegal entry into America is illegal and subject to immediate deportation. We are a nation of laws.
2. Every person here illegally has a deadline to come forward. This will be supported by new legislation that requires all employers to account for their employees.
3. No one will be allowed to work or receive taxpayer-funded services in America in an undocumented, illegal status.

4. Green cards, Visas, or employer documentation will be required to do anything in the country. An illegal person can do nothing in an illegal status.
5. Repeal the anchor baby law. Parents must be citizens for their children to be citizens.
6. For those already here, i.e., DACA etc. All who are eighteen years or older need to apply for citizenship; their fates settled with merit-based, case-by-case bases. Those under eighteen should go with their parents, or guardians, through the citizenship process.

Defund the Police

The consequences of this would be horrible. It is so ridiculous that I will only offer these:

1. A scenario.

Belittled law enforcement will quit or retire. Finding people willing to become officers will be difficult, and the consequences of lawlessness will cause us to come to our senses. Three Words: Wait for it.

2. A solution.

Community policing; Everyone eighteen to thirty years old from neighborhoods that desire dramatic changes in policing, is recruited to the police academy. All who qualify will primarily police their respective neighborhoods.

Problem solved? No, defunding the police is an awful idea.

Consider Christ ANEW and finish well, too. "Righteousness exalteth a nation: but sin is a reproach to any people" (Proverbs 14:34).

Death and Taxes: Double Trouble

"Deaths and hospitalizations rise as flu season hits full swing."[26]

"CNN poll: Most Americans oppose Trump's tax reform plan."[27]

"Trump's tax reform plan: Who are the winners and losers?"[28]

Wow! What a time we had in 2018. The flu peaked right around tax time, which was double trouble. From an early age, I remember people saying that there were two sure things: death and taxes. The joke being that death was the only way to escape taxes. Well, they were partially right. The truth is, there are ways to avoid taxes and while death does end personal taxation, the death and inheritance tax may apply to your relatives. The new tax overhaul has caused quite a stir, but what does your worldview provide as the perfect solution for death and taxes?

Now, the GOoD news (God's Good News): The King James Biblical worldview is that there are two sure things, death and judgment, and they are unintended acts of God. The God of Heaven does all things well. He created mankind to live and never die. God breathed life into man, thereby establishing a personal relationship and walk with God that is meant to be unending. Our choice to sin temporarily altered the plan. When we genuinely put our trust in Christ, the relationship is permanently reestablished.

Therefore, "And as it is appointed unto man once die and after this the judgment (Hebrews 9:27–28)."

All will die and spend eternity somewhere (Ecclesiastes 12:7).

And taxes? We are commanded to obey every authority. Taxes are temporal and though they can sting, the hurt is not permanent. As believers, we are to be good stewards of everything God has entrusted to us. Therefore, paying taxes glorifies God; Unfair taxation? Well, maybe. We live in a sin-cursed world. "Be angry, but sin not" (Ephesians 4:26–27).

Finally, if we live 121 years here, Whew! It will be nothing compared to eternity. Consider Christ ANEW. A million years from now, He will still be keeping all things new (Revelation 21:1–5).

"For he hath made him to be sin for us, who knew no sin; that we might be made the righteousness of God in him" (2 Corinthians 5:21).

"For if, when we were enemies, we were reconciled to God by the death of his Son, much more, being reconciled, we shall be saved by his life"(Romans 5:10).

"But he was wounded for our transgressions, he was bruised for our iniquities: the chastisement of our peace was upon him; and with his stripes we are healed" (Isaiah 53:5).

"For God hath not given us the spirit of fear; but of power, and of love, and of a sound mind"(2 Tim 1:7).

The God of Heaven has given everyone light. It is up to us to respond to that light by coming to Christ Jesus.

"That was the true Light, which lighteth every man that cometh into the world" (John 1:9).

Therefore, "Let your light so shine before men, that they may see your good works, and glorify your Father which is in heaven"(Matt 5:16).

This acronym is not unique to me but is all important: D.O.C.T.R.I.N.E.S. is essential; this is genuine Christianity in a nutshell. These precepts lift genuine Christianity above any other worldview; religious, or otherwise. Here is what the acronym represents:

D – Deity of Christ

God alone is able to create anything from nothing and forgive sins. The Lord Jesus is God.

"In the beginning was the Word, and the Word was with God, and the Word was God. The same was in the beginning with God. All things were made by him; and without him was not anything made that was made" (John 1:1–3).

"And the Word was made flesh, and dwelt among us, (and we beheld his glory, the glory as of the only begotten of the Father,) full of grace and truth" (John 1:14).

"I and my Father are one" (John 10:30).

"The Jews answered him, saying, 'For a good work we stone thee not; but for blasphemy; and because that thou, being a man, makest thyself God'" (John 10:33).

"And Thomas answered and said unto him, 'My Lord and my God'"(John 20:28).

"Jesus said unto them, 'Verily, verily, I say unto you, Before Abraham was, I am'" (John 8:58).

O –Original sin

In Adam, all became eternal living souls and all die because of disobedience.

"And the Lord God formed man of the dust of the ground, and breathed into his nostrils the breath of life; and man became a living soul" (Genesis 2:7).

"Then shall the dust return to the earth as it was: and the spirit shall return unto God who gave it" (Ecclesiastes 12:7).

"Behold, all souls are mine; as the soul of the father, so also the soul of the son is mine: the soul that sinneth, it shall die" (Ezekiel 18:4).

"Wherefore, as by one man sin entered into the world, and death by sin; and so death passed upon all men, for that all have sinned" (Romans 5:12).

"And when the woman saw that the tree was good for food, and that it was pleasant to the eyes, and a tree to be desired to make one wise, she took of the fruit thereof, and did eat, and gave also unto her husband with her; and he did eat" (Genesis 3:6).

C – Cannon of scripture

The King James Bible is the inerrant, absolute, authorized Bible for human beings. It is the Word of God revealed to mankind. Nothing else compares to it for answers in life, death, and decision making.

"All scripture is given by inspiration of God, and is profitable for doctrine, for reproof, for correction, for instruction in righteousness: That the man of God may be perfect, throughly furnished unto all good works" (2 Tim 3:16–17).

"For the prophecy came not in old time by the will of man: but holy men of God spake as they were moved by the Holy Ghost (2 Peter 1:21).

"Howbeit when he, the Spirit of truth, is come, he will guide you into all truth: for he shall not speak of himself; but whatsoever he shall hear, that shall he speak: and he will shew you things to come" (John 16:13).

"But the Comforter, which is the Holy Ghost, whom the Father will send in my name, he shall teach you all things, and bring all things to your remembrance, whatsoever I have said unto you" (John 14:26).

"Sanctify them through thy truth: thy word is truth" (John 17:17).

"Beloved, believe not every spirit, but try the spirits whether they are of God: because many false prophets are gone out into the world" (1 John 4:1).

"But there is a spirit in man: and the inspiration of the Almighty giveth them understanding" (Job 32:8).

"Knowing this first, that no prophecy of the scripture is of any private interpretation" (2 Peter 1:20).

"For the Holy Ghost shall teach you in the same hour what ye ought to say"(Luke 12:12).

T – Trinity

The Lord Jesus is God; the second person of the Godhead: God the Father (I AM), God the Son (Christ Jesus); God the Holy Ghost (Comforter and Holy Spirit).

"And God said, 'Let us make man in our image, after our likeness: and let them have dominion over the fish of the sea, and over the fowl of the air, and over the cattle, and over all the earth, and over every creeping thing that creepeth upon the earth'" (Genesis 1:26).

"For there are three that bear record in heaven, the Father, the Word, and the Holy Ghost: and these three are one" (1 John 5:7).

"I and my Father are one" (John 10:30).

"And the Word was made flesh, and dwelt among us, (and we beheld his glory, the glory as of the only begotten of the Father,) full of grace and truth" (John 1:14).

"And the Lord God said, 'Behold, the man is become as one of us, to know good and evil: and now, lest he put forth his hand, and take also of the tree of life, and eat, and live forever'" (Genesis 3:22).

"The grace of the Lord Jesus Christ, and the love of God, and the communion of the Holy Ghost, be with you all. Amen" (2 Corinthians 13:14).

"For in him dwelleth all the fulness of the Godhead bodily" (Colossians 2:9).

"Go to, let us go down, and there confound their language, that they may not understand one another's speech" (Genesis 11:7).

"Who being the brightness of his glory, and the express image of his person, and upholding all things by the word of his power, when he had by himself purged our sins, sat down on the right hand of the Majesty on high"(Hebrews 1:3).

"But when the Comforter is come, whom I will send unto you from the Father, even the Spirit of truth, which proceedeth from the Father, he shall testify of me" (John 15:26).

R –Resurrection

The Lord Jesus' resurrection conquered death for all who put their trust in Him. Eternal life is available to whosoever will repent and believe the Gospel (God's good news).

"Jesus said unto her, 'I am the resurrection, and the life: he that believeth in me, though he were dead, yet shall he live'" (John 11:25).

"For if we believe that Jesus died and rose again, even so them also which sleep in Jesus will God bring with him" (1 Thessalonians 4:14).

"And this is the will of him that sent me, that every one which seeth the Son, and believeth on him, may have everlasting life: and I will raise him up at the last day" (John 6:40).

"Therefore doth my Father love me, because I lay down my life, that I might take it again. No man taketh it from me, but I lay it down of myself. I have power to lay it down, and I have power to take it again. This commandment have I received of my Father" (John 10:17–18).

I – Incarnation

God took on flesh and became the perfect sacrifice that was required to make redemption possible for sinful mankind.

"For he hath made him to be sin for us, who knew no sin; that we might be made the righteousness of God in him" (2 Corinthians 5:21).

"And the Word was made flesh, and dwelt among us, (and we beheld his glory, the glory as of the only begotten of the Father,) full of grace and truth" (John 1:14).

"For the law was given by Moses, but grace and truth came by Jesus Christ" (John 17 and John 20:27–28).

N – New creation

The greatest evidence of salvation is a changed life.

"And I will give them one heart, and I will put a new spirit within you; and I will take the stony heart out of their flesh, and will give them an heart of flesh" (Ezekiel 11:19–20).

"Therefore if any man be in Christ, he is a new creature: old things are passed away; behold, all things are become new" (2 Corinthians 5:17).

"I am crucified with Christ: nevertheless I live; yet not I, but Christ liveth in me: and the life which I now live in the flesh I live by the faith of the Son of God, who loved me, and gave himself for me" (Galatians 2:20).

E – Eschatology

Christ Jesus will come again, put away sin, gather the saved, condemn the unbelievers to hell and establish His eternal, heavenly kingdom. This will result in the best form of government. Our representative republic is the best mankind can muster, but one day Christ Jesus will reign as the Righteous Dictator. You see, when the leadership is pure, perfect, holy and separate from in, the result is equality and justice—all the time.

> "For the Lord himself shall descend from heaven with a shout, with the voice of the archangel, and with the trump of God: and the dead in Christ shall rise first: then we which are alive and remain shall be caught up together with them in the clouds, to meet the Lord in the air: and so shall we ever be with the Lord. Wherefore comfort one another with these words" (1 Thessalonians 4: 16–18).

"For the invisible things of him from the creation of the world are clearly seen, being understood by the things that are made, even his eternal power and Godhead; so that they are without excuse"(Romans 1:20).

"For then shall be great tribulation, such as was not since the beginning of the world to this time, no, nor ever shall be" (Matthew 24:21–22).

"But the day of the Lord will come as a thief in the night; in the which the heavens shall pass away with a great noise, and the elements shall melt with fervent heat, the earth also and the works that are therein shall be burned up"(2 Peter 3:10).

"And if thy foot offend thee, cut it off: it is better for thee to enter halt into life, than having two feet to be cast into hell, into the fire that never shall be quenched" (Mark 9:45–48).

"But the fearful, and unbelieving, and the abominable, and murderers, and whoremongers, and sorcerers, and idolaters, and all liars, shall have their part in the lake which burneth with fire and brimstone: which is the second death" (Revelation 21:8). "And whosoever was not found written in the book of life was cast into the lake of fire" (Revelation 20:15).

S – Salvation

The Lord Jesus paid it all—His virgin birth, sinless life, death, burial, and resurrection provides redemption for the soul that believes.

"Verily, verily, I say unto you, He that heareth my word, and believeth on him that sent me, hath everlasting life, and shall not come into condemnation; but is passed from death unto life"(John 5:24).

"And I give unto them eternal life; and they shall never perish, neither shall any man pluck them out of my hand" (John 10:28).

"He that believeth on the Son of God hath the witness in himself: he that believeth not God hath made him a liar; because he believeth not the record that God gave of his Son"(1 John 5:10–13).

"That if thou shalt confess with thy mouth the Lord Jesus, and shalt believe in thine heart that God hath raised him from the dead, thou shalt be saved"(Romans 10:9).

"And this is the record, that God hath given to us eternal life, and this life is in his Son"(1 John 5:11–13).

"These things have I written unto you that believe on the name of the Son of God; that ye may know that ye have eternal life, and that ye may believe on the name of the Son of God"(1 John 5:13).

"For I delivered unto you first of all that which I also received, how that Christ died for our sins according to the scriptures; And that he was buried, and that he rose again the third day according to the scriptures"(1 Corinthians 15:3–4).

"For whosoever shall call upon the name of the Lord shall be saved" (Romans 10:13).

Again, DOCTRINE is all important when comparing worldviews. All other worldviews are found lacking when seeking solutions to every worldly issue when compared with The King James Biblical worldview.

God loves you. He desires a personal relationship with you that is real. He wants to be your Savior and your friend.

Chapter 5

Eternal Security vs. Economic and Homeland Security, The End of It All

"End of the world: Scientists send dire ocean tide warning"[29]

"Romanian billionaire and family dead after crashing plane in Milan"[30]

"Treasury Secretary Janet Yellen warns delay in raising debt limit will slow economy"[31]

THE TOP ONE percent that have, the needy, and personal responsibility; all come to mind when I think about these issues. That said, all of us will leave the same amount in the end; ALL OF IT.

"According to Christian numerologist David Meade the world will end on 23 Sept 2017"[32]

First of all, someone close to me once said, "Believe half of what you see and nothing that you hear." That means, do your homework and find out if any report is based on truth.

Now, the GOoD news (God's Good News): The King James Biblical worldview is that the rapture of the church is next in God's plan, followed by the tribulation and then one thousand good years. God created all things, and He will end it all by fire someday. "While the earth remaineth, seedtime and harvest, and cold and heat, and summer and winter, and day and night shall not cease" (Genesis 8:22). The good news is that whosoever will, can come to Him through Christ Jesus.

Why put your trust in Christ? We are not promised tomorrow down here in a sin cursed world but, we can have eternal life in heaven if we repent and believe the gospel.

"For all have sinned, and come short of the glory of God" (Romans 3:23).

"For I delivered unto you first of all that which I also received, how that Christ died for our sins according to the scriptures; And that he was buried, and that he rose again the third day according to the scriptures" (1 Corinthians 15:3–4).

"If we confess our sins, he is faithful and just to forgive us our sins, and to cleanse us from all unrighteousness" (1 John 1:9).

"For whosoever shall call upon the name of the Lord shall be saved" (Romans 10:13).

That said, does your worldview have the answer to the big three? Where did everything come from, what is our purpose for being here and, where are we going when we die? *Selah (Think on these things)*.

Conclusion: Fear not, this world will be here for a while; at least for one thousand, or more, years.

God loves you! He desires a personal relationship with you that is real. He wants to be your Savior and your friend.

Chapter 6

Faith, Feminism,
Food and Drug Safety, Foolishness

FAITH; IT IS only as good as its source. Without faith, it is impossible to please God; Fornication; the sin against self and God; Foolishness

"She Was 12-Years-Old and 9 Months Pregnant When She Disappeared Into The Cold December Night 25 Years Ago"[33]

"A Colorado Woman Who Refused COVID-19 Vaccine Because of Her Faith Is Denied Kidney Transplant"[34]

"Removing a condom without consent is now a violation of California's civil code"[35]

Wow, we are so removed from right that we've started making laws to support wrong.

If we back up and condemn fornication, most of our intimacy issues will be solved. God's design for intimacy in humans is one man and one woman for one lifetime in the marriage relationship. "Therefore shall a man leave his father and his mother, and shall cleave unto his wife: and they shall be one flesh" (Genesis 2:21–24).

Beginning and maintaining relationships, God's way, solves the communication issues surrounding pregnancy.

"How Clint Eastwood Really Feels About Religion"[36]

It is very important to be right about the existence of God. *OK; if meditation replaces religion; who or what are you meditating on, self? If there is no God, who or what are you meditating/relying on for help? If there is a God and you are not interested in His plan for mankind then; *Oh King live physically, in the here and now, forever; because this life is all you have. That said, why risk being separated from anything good for all of eternity when you die? At ninety-one years of age, Clint Eastwood had better be right.

What does your worldview offer for life after physical death? If you have any doubt about where you will spend eternity, my prayer is that you take *One Sincere Moment* and ask Him. Call out to the God of Heaven and He will answer.

Typically, we try to avoid calling each other fools as we all fall short of perfection, but:

"Birds aren't real and this man wants the world to know"[37]

Some things don't merit a response, although this comes to mind; Birdbrain, that said; the God of Heaven has something to say about foolishness:

"The fool hath said in his heart, There is no God. They are corrupt, they have done abominable works, there is none that doeth good" (Psalm 14:1).

"Answer not a fool according to his folly, lest thou also be like unto him. Answer a fool according to his folly, lest he be wise in his own conceit" (Proverbs 26:4–5).

Consider Christ ANEW, He gives wisdom when to answer and when to be quiet too.

"CNN's 'Catholic' Chris Cuomo: Americans don't 'need' help from above"[38]

What does your worldview offer for things to get better in this country? You see, professing to be "Christian" and being a genuine Christian are different.

The good news: Anyone who has died to self, repented of their sins, asked for forgiveness, and trusted Jesus Christ as their personal Lord and Savior is a Christian. This will show itself by what they do after repenting. "Therefore if any man be in Christ, he is a new creature: old things are passed away; behold, all things are become new" (2 Corinthians 5:17).

Christians are advised to be careful; we judge ourselves and then consider others. That said, we are commanded to be fruit inspectors. In others words, while we all are free to be wrong, we are just as free to recognize wrong and avoid the horrible consequences that follow. "Wherefore by their fruits ye shall know them"(Matthew 7:20).

Early on in my walk with Christ, an acronym was given to me: F.A.I.T.H. (Forsaking All I Trust Him). Along with this verse, Hebrews 11:6; these come to mind when I consider what genuine Faith is, as pleasing God is all important.

"But without faith it is impossible to please him: for he that cometh to God must believe that he is, and that he is a rewarder of them that diligently seek him" (Hebrews 11:6).

Our nation turning to God, though unlikely, is the only hope for a better country.

God loves you! He desires a personal relationship with you that is real. He wants to be your Savior and your friend.

Chapter 7

Grace, Gospel, Gender Identity, Global Warming

Grace and Truth, The Things of the God of Heaven are Perfectly Balanced

What does your worldview give as the origin of all things?

If you have gotten this far in this book, you've undoubtedly noticed a pattern at the end of each section. That is, "God loves you. And He desires a personal relationship with you that is real. He wants to be you Savior and your friend." It would be tragic of me not to mention God's amazing grace, in the "G" section when seeking solutions from A–Z.

The grace that He extends to all of us is remarkable. I learned this some time ago that Mercy is not giving us what we deserve; Grace is giving us more than we deserve. I have received His unmerited favor. The acronym G.R.A.C.E. comes to mind: God's Riches At Christ's Expense is available to all because He loves us so much. That said, the God of Heaven is right and just in everything He does and allows. Being rightly related to Him is the only solution for whatever hinders us.

God is so wonderful that I have coined the phrase, "2G is enough for me." Meaning, while some covet 3G, 4G, 4LTE or even 5G; All I need is to learn to Glorify God (2G) in everything I say, think and do. He provides the power I need to handle any of life's issues. All power belongs to Him. We can only succeed in this journey by repenting of our sins and trusting Jesus Christ as our personal Lord and Savior. Praise the Lord; I don't need 5G, 4LTE, or 3G. "2G" is enough for me. Glorify God.

"For by grace are ye saved through faith; and that not of yourselves: it is the gift of God: Not of works, lest any man should boast" (Ephesians 2:8–9).

"Woman Accused Of Using $4.9 Million Police Settlement To Buy Guns For Gang"[39]

"Out of the Darkness Walk 2017"[40]

"22-year-old woman killed after 12-year-old boy jumps from overpass in suicide attempt"[41]

The call for suicide awareness and prevention is noble, but what specific action does your worldview provide as the solution for suicides in America and around the world?

"On average, there are 121 suicides per day in the USA alone; even more alarming is that, on average, one person dies by suicide every 40 seconds somewhere in the world"[42]

Now, the GOoD news (God's Good News): The Christian, King James Biblical worldview is that all lives are special (Genesis 1:27–28 and Genesis 2:7). Self-worth is understood when one has a personal relationship with the Lord, Jesus Christ (Romans 8:16–17). While the accolades of this world are okay, our value is not determined by what we accomplish here or by the approval of others. The desire of the true believer is to glorify God; pleasing Him makes life worth living. What about the times we fall short? We have an advocate (1 John 2:1–2).

Christians are never hopeless or powerless. The solution to suicide is not found within, it is found in Christ (Ephesians 1:3–6). What we need is biblical revival, a genuine return to the Word of God, which answers a crucial question: What is our purpose for being here?

Trusting in Christ changes everything. It gives us a reason to live and instills praise and thankfulness to the One who gave us life (Ephesians 2:8–10).

When we understand that every life is unique and a precious gift from God, we cherish it. Consider Christ ANEW (Absolutely Nothing Else Works).

God loves you. He desires a personal relationship with you that is real. He wants to be your Savior and your friend.

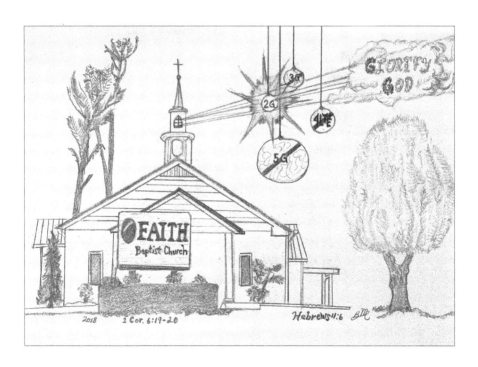

Chapter 8

Hath God Said, Hypocrisy and Holiness, per Lisa Simpson, "Prayer; the final desperate act of a scoundrel"

"Megachurch With Ferrari-Driving Pastor Gives Back $4.4M Pandemic Loan"[43]

HELL, ARE WE there yet? The homeless

This is the chapter I didn't look forward to writing as it reveals a great enemy; unbelief.

It is said in Christian circles (pun intended); that if we want revival, we should "Get a magic marker, bend down, and draw a circle around ourselves. While in the circle, look toward Heaven and ask the Lord: 'Please bring revival to this place; starting inside this circle.'"

You see, hypocrisy is rooted in unbelief. If we believed as we proclaimed, our actions would reflect our trust in Christ. I heard a great sermon by Pastor Dan Patterson on praying about everything. We should pray before saying or doing anything. Our actions, reactions, and consequences are changed for the better as a result. Become a POET (pray over every-thing) and know it.

"Be careful for nothing; but in every thing by prayer and supplication with thanksgiving let your requests be made known unto God. And the peace of God, which passeth all understanding, shall keep your hearts and minds through Christ Jesus" (Philippians 4:6–7).

The good news is forgiveness is available to all who sincerely pray, confess, and forsake their sins. Genuine believers need to have One Sincere Moment and examine themselves to continue to grow in faith until Christ returns or, calls us home.

"If we confess our sins, he is faithful and just to forgive us our sins, and to cleanse us from all unrighteousness" (1 John 1:9).

"Examine yourselves, whether ye be in the faith; prove your own selves. Know ye not your own selves, how that Jesus Christ is in you, except ye be reprobates?" (2 Corinthians 13:5).

That said, while believers struggle, fight, and get right, unbelievers are worse off: On a road to death and destruction; morning, noon, and night. Those who don't believe need One Sincere Moment to begin to get right.

"For the wages of sin is death; but the gift of God is eternal life through Jesus Christ our Lord" (Romans 6:23).

Hell is not hell because of the fire, beware. Hell is hell because God is not there.

Homelessness in America: really?

"Approximately a half-million people in the United States are homeless, with California accounting for 25 percent — the largest number of any state, according to a survey by the U.S. Department of Housing and Urban Development; Homeless encampments increasingly affecting California train traffic"[44]

"Facing backlash, California county rescinds homeless shelter plan"[45]

"National disgrace: Community fights back as California overrun by homelessness, human waste, needles"[46]

"Tiny homes for homeless veterans"[47]

What does your worldview give as a solution for ending homelessness in America?

It is amazing that we spend hundreds of millions on budgets, natural disasters and military aid to foreign nations; while homelessness in America still exists. I understand this has become a complicated issue and a lot more could be said.

Now, the GOoD news (God's Good News): Like most of our troublesome issues this is a sin problem. Homelessness is a consequence of people and cultures devoid of godly recognition and wisdom. Some are homeless due to bad choices, but others are victims and just desire a measure of peace in this sinned-cursed world.

"These things I have spoken unto you, that in me ye might have peace. In the world ye shall have tribulation: but be of good cheer; I have overcome the world" (John 16:33).

The essential thing is that all need to be rightly related to the Creator through Christ Jesus.

"For what shall it profit a man, if he shall gain the whole world, and lose his own soul? Or what shall a man give in exchange for his soul?" (Mark 8:36–37).

Again, no one should be homeless in America; but what about the freedom of those who want to live as they choose? Their freedom, as ours, ends where another citizen's nose begins. We are all in this together and therefore our lifestyles intermingle. Compassion and personal responsibility are essential. The sin of apostasy, rooted in unbelief, is the culprit.

Consider Christ ANEW and have an eternal home in Heaven too.

"Better is the poor that walketh in his uprightness, than he that is perverse in his ways, though he be rich" (Proverbs 28:6).

God loves you. He desires a personal relationship with you that is real. He wants to be your Savior and your friend.

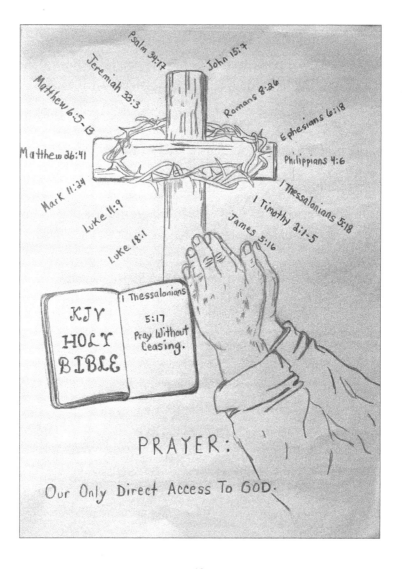

Chapter 9

ISOAR, In Christ Alone, Idol Worship, Introducing ISOAR

ISOAR IS THE culmination of several things I have been thinking about and praying over for some time now. It stems from my desire that you, and everyone, have abundant life in the here and now and a home in Heaven someday.

"Wait a minute," you may be saying. There other opinions as to what occurs in life and in death. Indeed, this is where ISOAR saves the day.

What would you say to a *solution* to our divisive culture? While we know difficult storms occur in life, what if we could be confident in the storm, knowing that we are going to make it to the other side? Welcome to ISOAR. You probably own several "I" products; an iPhone, iPad, etc. My personal favorite is iTarget Pro; I am former military and civilian Department of Defense (D.O.D) employee; enough said.

ISOAR is an interactive way to help us live a life that soars on eagles' wings. Which, is again, the most fulfilling and successful life possible. The acronym ISOAR breaks out to: "In Search Of Always Right." ISOAR compares worldviews while protecting liberty and justice for all.

Here are the important ground rules:

1) You and I must agree to be friends for the next twenty-one years or until death parts us. This frees us to interact personally, virtually, or anonymously; you choose. Relationships thrive when the parties involved get to know each other over time. The primary email address to message to participate is countdown21@

gmail.com. Please place ISOAR in the Subject line to join the conversation.

2) You must declare your personal worldview (you are free to have one, so name it). Any and every worldview is welcomed for comparison, from A (Agnosticism, Atheism) to Z (Zoroastrianism); we all have something, or someone, that formed what we believe and why we believe it.

3) We alternate asking, and answering, the important questions and issues of our day; using the *Rebate method of interaction. This is essential: any question posed is answered by both parties; you simply answer from your, personal, worldview. (Yes, "I don't know" is a valid answer, but is it best for everyone?) Keep searching because, what's right is out there.

4) Finally, compare your questions and answers to others and then choose wisely.

*Rebate: Generally, we think of a rebate as a portion of funds given back in retail sales. The ISOAR use is giving back what has been fed into our life in order to benefit others; when it's compared with someone else's worldview.

Again, what has been paid into your life is what you give to others. This is the opposite of "Debate," which we are accustomed to. While debate entails arguing and, often times debunking your opponent's stance, the goal of ISOAR is to provide answers and solutions to the questions of our day while having the other person's best interest at heart.

This leads to self-examination. Why do I believe what I believe? Where did I get my belief system from? Is it best for everyone?

It is important to understand that we can control our choices but not the consequences of sinful decisions. Again, the key is balance and desiring the best for others. Laying aside selfishness one issue at a time causes us to self-examine and choose what is right and best for everyone.

"But they that wait upon the LORD shall renew their strength; they shall mount up with wings as eagles; they shall run, and not be weary; and they shall walk, and not faint"(Isaiah 40:31).

Again, countdown21@gmail.com is where we begin. Place ISOAR in the subject line and finish well in the end. Thank you for being a blessing to others, and especially to me. All the best, God bless. Your friend forever (Ecclesiastes 12:13-14).

The King James Biblical worldview can be boiled down to this quote, "Mankind must be governed by God or they will be ruled by tyrants"– William Penn.

"Blackpink's Lisa breaks two Guinness records with solo debut Lalisa"[48]

"Nicole Thea, 24-year-old YouTube star, dies along with unborn child"[49]

Wow! When I consider these issues, my thoughts go in several directions. The first thing that comes to mind is selfishness. Someone put it this way; most of us suffer from a bad case of "Perpendicular-I-itus." That is, a severe case thinking only of oneself. Well, idol worship is alive and well. For instance, hooray for Hollywood; we have admiration for some individuals who are lost without God and hope in the world. We covet fame, riches, and material things. We need to see beyond ourselves and ask for help from the God who loves us.

The good news is: God helps those who help themselves? No, God helps those who die to self and live surrendered to Him. Yes, every loss of life is sad, but our admiration needs to be given to righteousness. All of our worship should be centered in Christ alone. One of the hardest things for sinful mankind to admit and say is, "I was wrong." Because we look for love and acceptance in all the wrong places, we suffer. Idol worship and fornication do not glorify God. Who, or what, does your worldview say we should worship?

God loves you. He desires a personal relationship with you that is real. He wants to be your Savior and your friend.

Chapter 10

Jesus Alone, It's all about Him, Just Say Yes to the Lord Jesus

"Paul McCartney wrote a play with John Lennon about JESUS … John said: Christianity will go. It will vanish and shrink…We're more popular than Jesus now"[50]

YET MORE OF the S.O.S. (Same Old Sin). Where is John Lennon today? He is dead, and has been since 1980 by the way. That said, as we are now, he once was; and he is now, we soon shall be. Christ Jesus, on the other hand, is alive and well. This is nothing new; denying the deity of Christ and claiming Christianity is on the way out is the same old sin, just a different day.

"Who is he that condemneth? It is Christ that died, yea rather, that is risen again, who is even at the right hand of God, who also maketh intercession for us"(Romans 8:34).

"Wherefore he is able also to save them to the uttermost that come unto God by him, seeing he ever liveth to make intercession for them" (Hebrews 7:25).

Understanding genuine or true Christianity is the key to knowing the God who loves you. I am amazed at what nonbelievers think Christianity is and even more shocked at what people who claim to be Christian think. This chapter will hopefully clear things a bit. We love Him (Jesus Christ) because He first loved us. True Christianity is a love affair. It all stems around what Christ has done and not what man must do. This is what separates Christianity from every other religion or invented idea of mankind. Genuine Christianity has a God who created it all. Every other common sense, atheistic idea, philosophy, or religion has a god created by man. Being a Christian means following the teachings of Christ. We can only do this by being spiritually born again and following His Word, The Holy Bible. The King James Bible is literally the mind of God revealed to mankind. It is everything God wants to say to us on this side of eternity. The King James Bible is the instruction book for the human being. It is historical, current, and futuristic. That is, it records events that have occurred, reveals our current condition, and reveals our eternal destiny. "Jesus Christ the same yesterday, and to day, and for ever" (Hebrews 13:8).

As my Pastor so eloquently preached, "He is the answer, just say yes to Jesus."

Just say yes to Jesus, Your Star put it on the bottom shelf,
It's the better of the two options; the other being pleasing self;
Just say yes to Jesus, It's down low so all can attain;
Listen to His still small voice; Come to Christ and be born again.
Just say yes to Jesus as your Pastor sings In Christ Alone;
God's Been Good; Lay your Isaac down before His throne.
Just say yes to Jesus, your Star is pulling for you;
Get all the way right with God; Have All this and Heaven too.
Just say yes to Jesus you've heard your Pastor declare,
He is The Answer; behold our God! Nothing can compare.

"In the beginning was the Word,…In him was life; and the life was the light of men" (John 1:1–4).

God loves you. He desires a personal relationship with you that is real. He wants to be your Savior and your friend.

Chapter 11

KJV Only

"These 15 Bible texts reveal why 'God's Own Party' keeps demeaning women."[51]

THIS ARTICLE IS so indicative of someone who is lost without God and hope in the world. This condition always leads to cherry picking and misinterpretation of the scriptures.

"Which things also we speak, not in the words which man's wisdom teacheth, but which the Holy Ghost teacheth; comparing spiritual things with spiritual. But the natural man receiveth not the things of the Spirit of God: for they are foolishness unto him: neither can he know them, because they are spiritually discerned"(1 Corinthians 2:13–14).

The reason I am a King James only believer is because it is the authorized Word of God. Again, it's the very mind of God revealed to mankind; the instruction book for human beings. My Pastor said it best: "Your Bible determines your beliefs, and your beliefs determine your behavior." What does your worldview provide as solution for every issue we face today?

"A Catholic reads the Bible."[52]

This article made me smile as it implied that reading the Bible is an unusual occurrence. The fact is, the act of faith is not important if the object of that faith is lacking. Again, I will put the King James Bible, by comparison, up against anything for accuracy and truth when applied to anyone's life. Did I mention that the King James Bible is the very mind of God revealed to mankind? It is the instruction book for human beings. It is the go-to for right, wrong, and truth; it the only resource to successfully live and die by. You may ask, "If the Bible really is the Word of God, why would He allow so many versions?"

Well, the good news; "Now the just shall live by faith: but if any man draw back, my soul shall have no pleasure in him" (Hebrews 10:38).

The God of Heaven knows our weaknesses. If He had miraculously made it impossible to change the Bible, mankind would be bowing down and worshiping the book. Additionally, freewill is required in a perfect love relationship, which is God's desire for us all. Therefore; God is able to say exactly what He means and is able to preserve His Word.

Again, the King James Bible is the authorized, cannon of Scripture for human beings. We need not add or take away from it.
"All scripture is given by inspiration of God, and is profitable for doctrine, for reproof, for correction, for instruction in righteousness" (2 Timothy 3:16).

What does your worldview give as the foundation for right, wrong, and absolute truth?

God loves you. He desires a personal relationship with you that is real. He wants to be your Savior and your friend.

And HE IS ...

HIGH PRIEST Hebrews 6:20
LIVING WATER John 6:35
BREAD OF LIFE John 6:51
SERVANT Matthew 20:28
ROCK 1 Corinthians 10:4
SHILOH Genesis 49:10
MASTER Matthew 23:10
ADVOCATE 1John 2:1
MESSIAH John 4:25-26
TRUE VINE John 15:1
SAVIOUR Acts 4:12
JUDGE Acts 10:42
ALPHA & OMEGA Revelation 22:13, ROSE OF SHARON Song of Solomon 2:1,
MAN OF SORROWS Isaiah 53:3, HEAD OF THE CHURCH Ephesians 5:23, LORD
OF LORDS 1 Timothy 6:15, SHEPHERD & BISHOP OF OUR SOULS 1 Peter 2:25,
THE RESURRECTION & THE LIFE John 11:25, AUTHOR & FINISHER OF OUR
FAITH Hebrews 12:2, IMAGE OF THE INVISIBLE GOD Colossians 1:15, LION OF
THE TRIBE OF JUDAH Revelation 5:5, WONDERFUL COUNSELOR Isaiah 9:6,
BRIGHT MORNING STAR Revelation 22:16, CHIEF CORNERSTONE Ephesians
2:20, LIGHT OF THE WORLD John 8:12, EVERLASTING FATHER Isaiah 9:6,
ONLY BEGOTTEN SON John 3:16, KING OF KINGS Revelation 19:16, KING OF
THE JEWS Mark 15:26, PRINCE OF PEACE Isaiah 9:6, GOOD SHEPHERD John
10:11, TEACHER Matthew 4:23, FAITHFUL & TRUE WITNESS Revelation 3:14, THE
ALMIGHTY Revelation 1:8, IAM John 8:58, BRANCH Isaiah 11:1
THE WORD John 1:1
THE DOOR John 10:9
HOLY ONE Mark 1:24
CARPENTER Mark 6:3
REDEEMER Job 19:25
DAYSPRING Luke 1:78
ANCHOR Hebrews 6:19
PROPHET Matthew 21:11
IMMANUEL Matthew 1:23
MEDIATOR 1 Timothy 2:5
LAMB OF GOD John 1:29
SON OF GOD Matthew 27:54
BRIDEGROOM Matthew 9:15
SON OF MAN Matthew 20:28
THE BELOVED Ephesians 1:6
THE AMEN Revelation 3:14
JEHOVAH Exodus 6:3; Psalm 83:18; Isaiah 12:2, 26:4
THE WAY, THE TRUTH & THE LIFE John 14:6

... THE LORD JESUS CHRIST!!

Chapter 12

Liars, Lottery,
and the Objects of Our Love

DAVID SAID IN his haste that all men are liars? Indeed he did, as recorded in Psalm 116:11. The follow-up question is; although he did it hastily, was he right? Yes indeed. Can your worldview produce anyone who has never lied?

"God forbid: yea, let God be true, but every man a liar; as it is written, That thou mightest be justified in thy sayings, and mightest overcome when thou art judged" (Romans 3:4).

Isn't it ironic that we are liars approximately sixteen hours of the day and then lie down (pun intended)? Our minds detach the other eight, or so, hours; oftentimes in restless sleep. A detached mind during sleep would be our only escape from our phony existence if not for God's grace. The good news is we have an advocate. God knows we are but flesh and although we don't escape the awful consequences of our sin, when we completely surrender to Him, repent and confess our sins; the lost person is converted and believers are restored, respectively.

"Men must be governed by God or they will be ruled by tyrants,"– William Penn

A common thing that identifies the lost liar is being scornful and using the Lord's name in vain. Actually, this is a blessing in disguise as the God of Heaven will be glorified in protest or in praise. Have you noticed that an unbelieving world can't eliminate God from the public conversation? Additionally, the believing liar is convicted and tormented due to a broken fellowship with their Creator who desires a close, loving, relationship. What does your worldview give as a solution for liars?

The Lottery, The Poor Man's Tax, He who seeks Riches

"Lottery winner dies with winning ticket still in his pocket"[53]

"California Man Wins Lottery 4 times in 6 Months For More Than $6 Million"[54]

Whatever the rationale: Hope scholarships, tax revenue, individuals seeking personal wealth etc.; Playing the lottery is wrong and should be avoided. There are two reasons I say no to lotteries:

1. For me to win, others have to lose. We are commanded to think of others. The ultimate desire being (via another acronym): "Oh, To Help Everyone Receive Salvation" (OTHERS).
2. It is not being a good steward of what God has blessed, and entrusted, us with (i.e. it's gambling).

There are bad consequences for gaining wealth in an ungodly fashion, it is sinful.

That brings me to the most important issue of this section. The good news is while nothing is wrong with being wealthy; the love of money always leads to failure. When the object of our Love is self, it leads to lies and the love of money always leads to heartache. The greatest life is achieved in a loving relationship with the Creator who loves you, Christ Jesus. What does your worldview give as the reason you love who or what you do?

"For the love of money is the root of all evil: which while some coveted after, they have erred from the faith, and pierced themselves through with many sorrows" (1 Timothy 6:10).

"Labour not to be rich: cease from thine own wisdom. Wilt thou set thine eyes upon that which is not? for riches certainly make themselves wings; they fly away as an eagle toward heaven" (Proverbs 23:4–5).

This said, rightly applied love is paramount. Our love for the One who gave Himself for us is essential.

If we love Him, we will listen to Him;
If we listen to Him, we will learn from Him,
If we learn from Him, we will live for Him,
If we live for Him, we will glorify Him,
If we glorify Him, we show everyone that we love Him.

"We love him, because he first loved us" (1 John 4:19).
"Greater love hath no man than this, that a man lay down his life for his friends" (John 15:13).

It doesn't matter who you are, or what you've done, God loves you. He desires a personal relationship with you that is real. He wants to be your Savior and your friend.

Chapter 13

Marriage, Alternative Lifestyles (Homophobia), Mass Shootings

"HOW UNMARRIED AMERICANS are changing everything.

Why aren't Millennials getting married?"[55]

A lot of reasons can be given for not marrying. I haven‹t met the right person; I'm not financially stable etc. My initial thought is that selfishness is the culprit. We live in a digital world that has become less relational. While marriage may not be practical to some, for the majority of us it is best. The reality is we all struggle with sharing. That said, in Vegas alone, more than a hundred marriages occur daily. I could give additional details but, what does your worldview give for the reason why millennials aren't getting married?

Now, the GOoD news (God's Good News): The Christian, King James Biblical, worldview is that our earthy marriages mirror the spiritual marriage between Christ and The Church (Ephesians 5:25–33); the Church being those who have, genuinely, trusted Jesus Christ as their personal Lord and Savior (Romans 10:10–13).

The desire to marry is God-given. Marriage is a covenant with God (Genesis 2:23–24) between one man and one woman and intended to last for a lifetime (Matthew 19:4–6).

Millennials are changing everything? Not really. This is nothing new (1 Timothy 4:1–3). Forbidding to marry; trying to hide from God, not marrying in a church, extreme diets, etc.; is the same old sin (SOS) inherited from the first Adam (Genesis 3:8). God's original plan and boundaries for intimacy remains unchanged. Shacking up, intimacy outside of the marriage relationship or, breaking the marriage covenant always leads to heartache and pain.

More good news: God says, "I love you," come to me just as you are, (Matthew 11:28) but "I love you" so much that "I won't leave you as you are" (2 Corinthians 5:17). Consider Christ ANEW.

Marriage is a God-given covenant between one man and one woman for life.

"Husbands, love your wives, even as Christ also loved the church, and gave himself for it;…Nevertheless let every one of you in particular so love his wife even as himself; and the wife see that she reverence her husband" (Ephesians 5:25–33).

The Rainbow Sign: The homosexual and transgender agenda on the wrong side of "HIS-Story."

"North Carolina Lt. Gov. Refuses to Resign After Calling LGBTQ Community: Filth."[56]

"Dave Chappelle sparks LGBTQ+ controversy again."[57]

Indeed, this article addresses that genders are, in fact, different. Every person comes from a woman. Men and women are unique. This is one of the few times I agree with a comedian. That said, the consequences that result from sinful behavior is not a laughing matter.

"Playboy releases October cover featuring a man dressed in women's lingerie and heels."[58]

"Australia votes yes to same-sex marriage."[59]

"Oklahoma woman who married mother after two 'hit it off' leads guilty to incest."[60]

"Transgender people will be allowed to enlist in the military as court case advances."[61]

A lot is said about equal rights, but ultimately it comes down to right and wrong, choices, and consequences. Homophobia you say? Well, genuine Christians don't fear homosexuals; we are afraid of what their future holds. You see, we all have the right to be wrong. We control our choices but, who or what will determine the consequences?

We are presently in the midst of an attempt to persuade everyone to accept alternative lifestyles. For instance, "Gay penguins raise newly hatched chick at New York zoo."[62]

This is, extremely, ridiculous. This indoctrination is destined for failure as the God of Heaven protects His people.

What does your worldview give as the end result of a world void of traditional relationships and gender absolutes?

Now, the GOoD news (God's Good News): The Christian, King James Biblical worldview is that, while sincere, we can be sincerely wrong. Calling good bad and bad good is nothing new. When God saw mankind and that the "thoughts of his heart was only evil continually," He intervened (Genesis 6:5–7).

We are not your own; Christ Jesus died for everyone; therefore, our purpose for being here is to glorify Him. "For ye are bought with a price: therefore glorify God in your body, and in your spirit, which are God's" (1 Corinthians 6:20).

How ironic that the very symbol (the "bow in the cloud") used as a rallying cry for equality is actually a sign of mercy; a grace period (Genesis 9:11–15). Ultimately, it is a warning sign of pending judgment (2 Peter 3:3–10).

This is merely a continuation of moral decline; it is the Same Old Sin (SOS) different day.

Flashback: Remember, don't ask don't tell? The following is what I recorded (unedited) in 2010:

Claiming the reported presidential victory for Barack Obama, the repealing of don't ask don't tell, is a bit premature. The consequences are yet to come. Don't take my word for it, just wait, watch, and see. Actually, the policy was doomed to fail from the start. Secular wisdom is so flawed that it completely misses the mark.

It (secular wisdom) didn't even come up with the better answer, don't ask don't tell, across the board. That is, sexual preference should not be a factor in the workplace for anyone, straight, gay, or other-wise. The military, like all other jobs, has a work to do. Who cares what someone's sexual orientation is? Do your job and shut up about your sex life. Herein is the problem. Secular wisdom misses the best answer. The eight-hundred-pound gorilla in the room is the fact that homo-sexuality is wrong and will never be right even if you, me, and the rest of the world condone it. The sad truth is that the homosexual lobby is looking for a degree of acceptance that can never be realized. There happens to be a God in heaven that always has the last word, and He says homosexuality is not something new, progressive, or wise. It is sin.

It must be said that homosexuality is no worse than any other sin, but God hates all sin. Therefore, the consequences are guaranteed to be unfavorable as no sin goes unpunished, just as no good deed goes unrewarded. God is sovereign, right, and just in everything He does and allows.

Well, since we claim to be "one nation under God," but deny the power of God, don't ask don't tell was doomed from the start. We didn't have a foundation for truth. Therefore, the result is error; for the record, December 23, 2010. Dear Lord, in your wrath, have mercy on us.

God loves us as we are, but he loves us so much that he refuses to leave us the way we are. Love relationships are only perfected when they are reciprocal and unconditional. "We love him because he first loved us" (1 John 4:19).

"But God commendeth his love toward us, in that, while we were yet sinners, Christ died for us" (Romans 5:8). Anyone who comes to God and genuinely repents of their sins, is forgiven and their life is changed forever, for the better (2 Corinthians 5:17–21).

While we are free to choose and accept alternative lifestyles, the consequences are not good. Again, no sin goes unanswered. The God of Heaven made them male and female (Genesis 1:26–27).

"Therefore shall a man leave his father and his mother, and shall cleave unto his wife: and they shall be one flesh" (Genesis 2:21–24). No exceptions, God designed it that settles it. Consider Christ ANEW, only the Christian lifestyle will do.

"I will praise thee; for I am fearfully and wonderfully made: marvellous are thy works; and that my soul knoweth right well" (Psalm 139:14).

"40 Shot During Weekend in Mayor Lori Lightfoot's Chicago."[63]

"Why does the Las Vegas shooter's motive even matter?"[64]

"Texas church massacre: Timeline of US church shootings."[65]

"The horror of Las Vegas and the hope of heaven, Pastor Robert Jeffress."[66]

"8 killed in mass shooting at Indianapolis FedEx facility; suspect, 19, was former employee."[67]

"AT least seven are dead after a gunman opened fire at a birthday party in a Colorado Springs trailer park where children were present."[68]

The NPR report stated that, on average, a mass shooting occurs daily in the United States. That is a single event causing four or more deaths by firearm. The typical, possible causes/solutions were addressed: The U.S. gun culture, gun control, mental health, etc. Additionally, the pastor's message about the hope of heaven and believing doesn't offer details about God's requirements. That said, I asked for social media help in identifying the important issues of our time. One of the first responses I received was, "No respect for human life." The horrible event in Vegas should have started conversations about all human life (i.e. murder, abortion, euthanasia, suicides, etc.), but the immediate rush was to gun control.

Now, the GOoD news (God's Good News): The Christian, King James Biblical worldview is that every life lost is a mass casualty (2 Peter 3:9). That is, every life, born or unborn, is precious to God. Our problem is this unfortunate truth: The human heart is naturally flawed (Jeremiah 17:9). We are a fallen race; Sinners that fall short of the mark, which is perfection (Romans 5:12). The really good news is that anyone can turn from their sins, receive Christ, and be forgiven. That done, then they begin to have all others best interest at heart, which is the only solution (2 Corinthians 5:17).

In this sin cursed world of evil, which includes gun violence, truth is all important. While God's grace is available to all, the Gospel is only good news to those who genuinely trust Jesus Christ as their personal Lord and Savior. The Gospel is absolute truth and is bad news to all who reject it and die in trespasses and sins. The answer for mankind is a changed heart. You must be born again. Life is good but, eternal life is better. Again, the solution to our murderous, immoral ways is a change of heart and to be rightly related to our Creator (Proverbs 3:5–6).You see, the wicked heart respects no laws and will find a way to commit wrongs while the righteous heart respects all life and will want what's best for others (Ephesians 2:8–9).

What does your worldview provide as the solution for mass shootings?

Consider Christ ANEW. Read Romans 12:9–10.

God loves you. He desires a personal relationship with you that is real. He wants to be your Savior and your friend.

Chapter 14

Natural Born Sinners, Nasty by Nature, NFL Protest

"Teen wrote note begging family 'not to be ashamed' before taking her own life."[69]

IT'S SO SAD when suicide becomes the solution. It is so important to have a solid foundation for why mental issues occur. We are all natural born sinners living in a sin-cursed world.

We need an advocate, someone to offer hope for today and tomorrow. His name is the Lord Jesus. He says, "Come unto me, all ye that labour and are heavy laden, and I will give you rest" (Matthew 11:28).

We all have the right to be wrong.

"Do you agree, disagree, with Donald Trump's comments on NFL player protests?"[70]

This really took off, but why? Everyone seems to agree that all are free to peacefully protest and that should include The President. An office shouldn't limit anyone's right to agree or disagree. That said, now the GOoD news (God's Good News): The King James Biblical worldview is that we, true Christians, aren't protesting anything; we are promoting Christ Jesus (Matthew 11:28).

If we, as individuals or a nation, are ever going to rid ourselves from the curse of the past and unite as one it will be accomplished God's way. Here's the gist: Slavery is an awful sin. Unforgiveness is an awful sin. It is important that we live in the present. While we reject wrong, and promote prosecuting it to the full extent of the law, we must be willing to unconditionally forgive.

Unforgiveness is the major/current sin in this issue (Ephesians 4:31–32).

What does your worldview give as a solution to this issue?

Conclusion: What's needed is a change of heart on all sides (Romans10:9–10).

Consider Christ ANEW (Absolutely Nothing Else Works). God's law supersedes man's law.

God loves you. He desires a personal relationship with you that is real. He wants to be your Savior and your friend.

Chapter 15

One "In Christ" Is the Majority, One Sincere Moment

"Americans are in a mental health crisis — especially African-Americans. Can churches help?"[71]

"In U.S., Decline of Christianity Continues at Rapid Pace, An update on America's changing religious landscape."[72]

WELL, THIS SECTION could go in several directions. Genuine Christians never consider themselves a minority as we are joint heirs with Christ, and He owns it all. That said, the decline noted in the article is misleading. It is impossible for genuine Christianity to decline. We believe in the eternal security of the believer and the insecurity of the make believer.

For instance, my pastor mentioned that two of the major reasons people leave a local church is due to financial or dress code issues. You see, these two issues often expose the make believe Christian. Genuine believers trust God and tithe because it is biblical. They know they are stewards of money and support the local church because the God of Heaven owns it all. Genuine believers desire to give God their best; Men in a man's attire, women in woman's attire. This is important because God says so.

This sin cursed world culture is trying to indoctrinate us into believing a lie. There is a difference between men and women, and alternative lifestyles are wrong and will never be right. By the way, the church does not have a dress code—anyone can come. But know this, real preachers will preach what God says.

"The woman shall not wear that which pertaineth unto a man, neither shall a man put on a woman's garment: for all that do so are abomination unto the Lord thy God"(Deuteronomy 22:5).

It is up to us to trust and obey. Again, make believe Christians leave the local church. True believers desire to get all the way right with God. They stay in church and continue to make things better and strive to personally, do better.

"They went out from us, but they were not of us; for if they had been of us, they would no doubt have continued with us: but they went out, that they might be made manifest that they were not all of us" (1 John 2:19).

Scripture tells us that things will worsen before our God, Christ Jesus, returns to make all things right.

The power and purpose of One

We are One nation under God (even in Apostasy, moral awfulness, political anarchy).

One man, One woman, One Lifetime is the only real marriage.

There's only One God, One Mediator; The Lord Jesus Christ; He said "I am The Way" (John 14:6).

All of the aforementioned secures an abundant life; we only get One chance at it.

What does your worldview offer as the solution for what is the best life for everyone?

The good news: By one man (Adam) sin enslaved all, but by one Man (the Lord Jesus), all can be free. Again, what is needed is *One Sincere Moment* to genuinely call out to God for help. We all need an honest self-examination and accept the reality that we all fall short; we are in need of a Savior.

"For God sent not his Son into the world to condemn the world; but that the world through him might be saved"(John 3:17).

We all must have a desire to be saved. It only takes *One Sincere Moment* to understand our hopeless condition and then repent and believe the Gospel. Eternal life is offered to everyone. The God of Heaven lovingly reaches out to us, but again we have to respond because love relationships are only perfected when they are reciprocal and, unconditional.

I am so thankful that the God of Heaven convicted me when, in my lost condition, I had *One Sincere Moment* and cried out, "Oh God, if you are up there, I want to know you."

"Ask, and it shall be given you; seek, and ye shall find; knock, and it shall be opened unto you: For every one that asketh receiveth; and he that seeketh findeth; and to him that knocketh it shall be opened" (Matthew 7:7–8).

God loves you. He desires a personal relationship with you that is real. He wants to be your Savior and your friend.

Chapter 16

Pledge Allegiance, PRICE of Freedom, Pride is Number One On God's Hate List, Poems

"Michigan redistricting committee rejects Pledge of Allegiance at meetings: To divisive"[73]

I PLEDGE ALLEGIANCE?

In the aftermath of the unfortunate death of George Floyd, there appears to be a continuous downhill slide concerning patriotism. This question was posed recently: "The Pledge of Allegiance; is it True or False?" Actually, this is an outstanding question. Well, as with everything, it comes down to your worldview. Who or what are to listening to? Can your worldview provide a solution to this and every question or issue that comes your way?

Let's break it down: "I pledge allegiance to the flag of the United States of America..."

The key is "I." It's an individual choice and the first indication that the pledge is true. We can love America, hate it, and leave it too.

"And to the Republic for which it stands,"

America is also a Republic, a representative one at that. Again, we are free to vote and represent America in the military, and in public/

civilian service. The alternative is to go and live under socialism, communism, or some other ungodly dictatorship. I've lived in several countries abroad; none were as free, just, or less racist than America.

"One nation, under God, indivisible, with liberty and justice for all." Therefore, the best leadership or government would have righteous statutes and laws, and would enforce them accordingly. Again, each individual remains free to choose but the governmental stance should be one of righteousness. This is impossible without a sure foundation for what is right and wrong.

Now, the GOoD news (God's Good News): We're under God whether we like it or not, but unity only happens when we do our part by living God's way. Additionally, a pure, perfect, and Holy God cannot coexist with imperfection. Therefore, no sin goes unpunished. He is a just God. If we say, or live as if, there is no God, we have to live with the consequences. How are we doing in the United States today? Fortunately for sinful mankind, Christ Jesus died for us in order that we can really live.

"Come unto me, all ye that labour and are heavy laden, and I will give you rest" (Matthew 11:28).

"For when we were yet without strength, in due time Christ died for the ungodly" (Romans 5:6).

Living God's way includes loving, living, and forgiving.

1. Love your neighbor as yourself. This works for the public and law enforcement too.

"Honour thy father and thy mother: and, Thou shalt love thy neighbour as thyself" (Matthew 19:19).

2. Live righteously before a pure, perfect, and Holy God. Thereby, finding favor with God and man; this includes law enforcement officers. When we live to please our Creator, we don't have to worry about being profiled.

"For the grace of God that bringeth salvation hath appeared to all men, Teaching us that, denying ungodliness and worldly lusts, we should live soberly, righteously, and godly, in this present world; Looking for that blessed hope, and the glorious appearing of the great God and our Saviour Jesus Christ; Who gave himself for us, that he might redeem us from all iniquity, and purify unto himself a peculiar people, zealous of good works" (Titus 2:11–14).

3. Forgive everyone; Black, White, Red, or Blue; all the way back to Adam too. Leave strife alone and move on. Again, one of the greatest sins hindering minorities is the sin of unforgiveness.

"And be ye kind one to another, tenderhearted, forgiving one another, even as God for Christ's sake hath forgiven you" (Ephesians 4:32).

"Then came Peter to him, and said, Lord, how oft shall my brother sin against me, and I forgive him? till seven time? Jesus saith unto him, I say not unto thee, Until seven times: but, Until seventy times seven" (Matthew 18:21–22).

That said, none of the above can be accomplished on your own. You must be born again; being rescued from death to life and freed from the bondage of sin by trusting Jesus Christ as your personal Lord and Savior.

"For whosoever shall call upon the name of the Lord shall be saved" (Romans 10:13).

You see, sons and daughters of the one true God, Christ Jesus, are completely free because they are not seeking approval from you or me. They give their allegiance to the one who died for them. Subsequently, their eyes are open to the King James biblical worldview, which includes obeying every authority, which in turn makes them love and live peaceably with all others too.

"Obey them that have the rule over you, and submit yourselves: for they watch for your souls, as they that must give account, that they may do it with joy, and not with grief: for that is unprofitable for you" (Hebrews 13:17).

Finally, the only thing that supersedes man's law is God's Word, which reveals His law. Genuine, peaceful protests are not sinful as they are lawful, but again, God knows the intent of the heart and no sin goes unpunished. Leaders and law enforcement are subject to God's authority also.

"When the righteous are in authority, the people rejoice: but when the wicked beareth rule, the people mourn" (Proverbs 29:2).

Well, there you have it, the biblical worldview. Compare it to yours.

What are you pledging allegiance to?

The PRICE for Freedom
All gave some, some gave all, but only One died and arose again for all.

The underlying cause of lack of patriotism is pride, which is love of self as opposed to love of country. The good news: Consider Christ ANEW and be completely free too.

P–atriotism
R–ewarding success
I–ndividual responsibility
C–ompassion
E–ternal security

"After family members contracted COVID-19, Ozzy Osbourne says worshiping Satan protected him from virus."[74]

The devil protected me? Pride comes before a fall, wait for it. There is only one way out of the coming judgment for such foolishness and that is to never physically die.

"And the times of this ignorance God winked at; but now commandeth all men every where to repent" (Acts 17:28–31).

Here are a few poems I wrote:

The sound of Angel wings
The part of a choir song when only women sing;
The sound of Bible pages right before the message man of God brings.
Giving credit where credit is due: Thank you Lord, it's all you.

TWAS THE NIGHT BEFORE "LIFE"
Twas the night before CHRISTmas and all through the land,
Not a righteous person is found; just sin on every hand.
The shephards are watching their flocks by night,
When out of the darkness comes a Great Light.
The Light that lights every man, woman, boy and girl,
That's born; then again when they die to this world.
The Lord Jesus offers, in a world full of strife,
Merry CHRISTmas to all and to all Eternal Life – (1 John 5:12)

You Are A Preacher
In this world we live in, it is difficult today
To be the Man of God, behind a pulpit and say:
You are a sinner, from beginning to end,
Repent, believe The Gospel, and life will begin.
Don't you know You are a Preacher;
Your life is a Pulpit, You are the leader.
Yes, You are a teacher; You choose the lesson plan,
You life leads the way, others watch and consider your stand,
Pop quiz: Is what you say, what you display;
What determines your answers today?

The Beauty that is unique to real Christianity
It's whosoever will, even if many won't.
So whosoever doesn't is free, don't.
Willingly a bondservant of Jesus Christ
I am commanded to go;
Just as free to suggest, Consider Christ,
As you are to say, no.
Now, you are without excuse, being educated,
Simply stated; Love is perfected when freely reciprocated.
"We love him, because he first loved us" (1 John 4:19).

True Love, Wrote December 3, 1999
True love is opening your heart and letting Christ in,
Then starting all over again,
To know joy so grand you lose all fear,
Seeing confusing things so clear,
Knowing that true happiness comes from the giving,
Understanding the real reason you're living,
To care, share, and sacrifice,
To do all this and not think twice,
To always know things will get better,

Knowing what things really matter,
God, your salvation, your family, then yourself,
With plenty of room in your heart for everything else,
Friends, neighbors, people on the street,
Any of God's children you might happen to meet,
Being thankful in the morning and at lights out,
That's what true love is all about.

This next poem can be sung to the music of the song "My Favorite Things" from the Roger and Hammerstein musical, *The Sound of Music*:

Sundays in Sunday school singing in Choir,
Preaching that reveals, there's an escape from the fire,
The assurance of salvation that redemption brings,
This is the list of my most favorite things.
When the trials come, when the storms rage,
When the evil one tries to sting,
I simply remember my Saviour and sing,
He's The Best Thing!

Retirement has been wonderful. This is the poem I penned upon retiring in 2014.

Retirement parting shot: Hanging up the "SIGINT" sweater.
Oh how amazing it is
To issue this bitter sweet letter,
I'm hanging up my GUHOR stick
Retiring my SIGINT sweater,
No swapping kids in parking lots
Badging in and out,
No touring the basement
In search of a shorter route,
Lesson learned along the way

In defending "In God We Trust:"
The monitoring of all others
Is proper and a must,
Yes, giving up the reel-to-reels
Morse code and paper tape,
My delta-data computing
On mid-shift when it's late,
When bleeding profusely
And coffee just won't do,
Nodding off on a day shift
It's time for a younger crew,
I'll miss the casual Fridays
The pig-ins and outs for sure,
Many co-workers along the way
No worries, the mission is secure,
How wonderful it is
As sweet outweighs the bitter,
I'm spared spinning and grinning
For Facebook, Skype and Twitter,
No more 3:21am alarm clocks
No more being tied to the rack,
No looking for 1D10Ts
Seeking Patriots to attack,
Through teary eyes and smiling lips
Brainstorming revealed this angle,
I'm so short I can sit on a curb
And my feet can finally dangle!
Cheers, I'm GFTD-uration.. Bill
p.s. Oh yeah, the most important thing:

"Honour all men. Love the brotherhood. Fear God. Honour the king" (1 Peter 2:17).

God loves you. He desires a personal relationship with you that is real. He wants to be your Savior and your friend.

Chapter 17

Question, question, questions, Quiet Please, Be Still and Know

"Questions To Ask Yourself Before Starting An Open Relationship."[75]

HUMOR? A LIFE that glorifies sinful behavior is not funny.

If you've gotten this far in the book and remain a skeptic, wait for it. It's only a matter of time before all will become clear. Again, do you have an answer to these three all important questions?

Where did you come from?

What is your purpose for being here?

Where are you going when you die?

Before you reconsider these questions (above), consider seeking honest answers to them. Try using the Rebate method. You see, we are accustomed to debate: Considering something; deliberating and engaging in arguments by discussing opposing points.

Again, I suggest a more revealing and helpful method, the rebate. Yes, this is a play on words, but the results are amazing. You see a rebate deducts or returns (an amount) from a payment or bill. How is this applied to our relationships? Well, we rebate (versus debate) by giving back what's been paid into our lives. That is, we share what has formed our personal worldview and compare it to other worldviews. As for me, I have a King James biblical worldview and will gladly compare it with any belief system. If you haven't already, see the ISOAR, chapter nine, for the method of using answers instead of arguments, for the way to truth and solutions.

Also, the art of being quite can be helpful. Being still allows us to self-examine and makes space available to hear from the Creator of all things.

"James Webb Telescope show Big Bang didn't happen?"[76]

Now back to the three very important questions. Compare your answers to these.

1) Where did you come from?
The God of Heaven, Christ Jesus, created all things including you and me.

"In the beginning God created the heaven and the earth" (Genesis 1:1).

"All things were made by him; and without him was not any thing made that was made" (John 1:3).

"So God created man in his own image, in the image of God created he him; male and female created he them" (Genesis 1:27).

2) What is your purpose for being here?
Under God's amazing umbrella of love, there are two great pillars that all of life's issues fall under. Those are discovery and sacrifice.

Discovery: You see, mankind has never created anything. We have only advanced by discovering what's already possible. Only the God of Heaven is able to create something from nothing. Thankfully, even though we fall desperately short and are undeserving, He loves us unconditionally and blesses our efforts.

"It is the glory of God to conceal a thing: but the honour of kings is to search out a matter" (Proverbs 25:2).

Thus, the reason I am all for scientist to keep on seeking. Eventually, they will discover and agree with what the God of Heaven has revealed in His Word, The King James Bible.

Sacrifice: Discovering our purpose for being here requires sacrifice (pun intended). The first thing that has to be sacrificed is self. We have to die to self and turn to God, in Christ Jesus. Additionally, every successful relationship between individuals, including marriages, workers, politicians etc., requires sacrifice. Ultimately, the greatest sacrifice occurred at the cross and the empty tomb.

"For I delivered unto you first of all that which I also received, how that Christ died for our sins according to the scriptures; And that he was buried, and that he rose again the third day according to the scriptures:" (1 Corinthians 15:3–4).

Our ultimate purpose for being here is to glorify God and enjoy Him forever.

3) Where are you going when you die? We all will spend eternity somewhere.

"And the LORD God formed man of the dust of the ground, and breathed into his nostrils the breath of life; and man became a living soul" (Genesis 2:7).

"Then shall the dust return to the earth as it was: and the spirit shall return unto God who gave it" (Ecclesiastes 12:7).

"And as it is appointed unto men once to die, but after this the judgment" (Hebrews 9:27).

Again, how does your worldview address the critical issues of our day?

Christ Jesus is the answer if you have a question. If you have all the answers, you are self-righteous.

The Lord Jesus says, "I came not to call the righteous, but sinners to repentance" (Luke 5:32).

God loves you. He desires a personal relationship with you that is real. He wants to be your Savior and your friend.

Chapter 18

Racism, The Art of the Rebate vs. Debate (see ISOAR), Righteousness and Peace, Resurrection, a Must, Remember

"Sporting legend Michael Jordan donated $10 million to open health clinics in his hometown of Wilmington."[77]

It is great to see successful individuals giving back.

"Render therefore to all their dues: tribute to whom tribute is due; custom to whom custom; fear to whom fear; honour to whom honour" (Romans 13:7).

"Black People Formed One of the Largest Militias in the U.S. Its Leader Is In Prosecutors Crosshairs."[78]

NFAC, THE NOT (vulgarity) Around Coalition; this is wicked and another indication that God's Word is so right. The use of profanity in the title of this group is a giveaway without even knowing their actions. And while some will say "we are not to judge," we are to be fruit inspectors. Something is rotten here.

"Wherefore by their fruits ye shall know them" (Matthew 7:20).

Ultimately, the sin of pride and unforgiveness is the culprit here.

"Joy Behar Says Black People Shouldn't Be Scared Of COVID Vaccine Anymore Because White People Were TheExperiment."[79]

"Schools across America launch BLM week of action featuring four controversial national demands."[80]

"Brian Flores tells CNN his kids were inspiration to file lawsuit against NFL and 3 teams alleging racial discrimination."[81]

"New York City mayor apologizes for calling white cops crackers."[82]

It is sad how the issue of race in so emphasized, but it is not surprising as it is a result of sin and unbelief. When nations or individuals don't have a solid foundation for right and wrong, they err. This includes all sides of the issue. The result is a troubled life without peace. Again, racists are wrong for hating and those who feel oppressed are wrong for not forgiving and forgetting.

"There is no peace, saith the LORD, unto the wicked" (Isaiah 48:22).

"For there is one God, and one mediator between God and men, the man Christ Jesus"(1 Peter 2:5).

"And be ye kind one to another, tenderhearted, forgiving one another, even as God for Christ's sake hath forgiven you" (Ephesians 4:32).

Now, the GOoD news (God's Good News): In Christ Jesus there is unity.

"There is neither Jew nor Greek, there is neither bond nor free, there is neither male nor female: for ye are all one in Christ Jesus" (Galatians 3:28).

What does your worldview give as the answer to racism?

As for war; peace and righteousness have kissed each other. There can be no peace without righteousness.

"Mercy and truth are met together; righteousness and peace have kissed each other" (Psalm 85:10).

There aren't any peaceful nations in a sin cursed world.

"Righteousness exalteth a nation: but sin is a reproach to any people" (Proverbs 14:34).

Christ's life, death, burial, and resurrection is the remedy. Without Him we are lost and without hope in this sin-sick world.

Self-examination is essential. We need to stop being overly busy with the things of this world as they are temporary. I often state: We all leave the same amount when we die, all of it.

"Be still, and know that I am God: I will be exalted among the heathen, I will be exalted in the earth" (Psalm 46:10).

Remember? Pun intended; I've learned to appreciate the ability to remember as I've aged, but there are times that forgetting is appropriate. It's said that we should remember our past in order to not repeat our mistakes. On the surface this appears to be a good statement, but it fails to consider the heart of mankind. Without a changed heart it is impossible for us to respond appropriately to trials, tests, trouble, and temptations. Additionally, we never fully understand the potential for blessings through it all.

Undoubtedly, the most profound statement ever made is: "In the beginning God created the Heaven and the earth" (Genesis 1:1).

Considering Genesis 1:1 encouraged me to list some other profound statements that confirm my worldview. This is my very, very long prayer, and meditation, list of things to remember:

Remember, Prayer is our only direct access to God.

Remember, All Gave Some, Some Gave All, but Only ONE, Christ Jesus, Died for the Enemy.

Remember, your best day as a Christian should be today.

Remember, Backsliding ends when knee bending begins.

Remember, But for the grace of God, we would not be…to include being here (period).

Remember, When saved; God does not see you as you were; He doesn't see you as you are, He sees you as He is.

Remember, "The world has yet to see what God can do with a man fully consecrated to Him…" – Dwight L. Moody

Remember to Trust in the Lord with all thine heart; He will direct your paths.

Remember, Memory is a luxury only a saved man can enjoy.

Remember, The devil can beat us on the outside but salvation has sealed us from within.

Remember, Sound D.O.C.T.R.I.N.E.

Remember, Do everything for His Glory.

Remember, He made it ALL; He owns it ALL.

Remember, the law is good if used lawfully and sets us free to Love our first Love.

Remember God in the wilderness; meditate in the night watches.

Remember what God has forgotten; my iniquity He remembers no more.

Remember to **Please Remember 'I' Destroys Everything** (PRIDE).

Remember to remember DOCTRINE is an essential.

Remember to rejoice, attitude signifies gratitude.

Remember that the things of God are perfectly balanced.

Remember to see you as He sees you. Remember you are a miracle, uniquely made for a personal love relationship with God.

Remember to remember preaching. It is what God uses to make significant changes in your life.

Remember who He (the God of Heaven) is.

Remember to pray without ceasing.

Remember, you don't know everything about God. We only know what's been revealed and that's enough.

Remember He healed them all.

Remember to invest in the things of God in your home.

Remember, the God of Heaven in hard times and react appropriately. Go back to the Word of God.

Remember to remember Heaven and Hell are real. Get excited and really live.

Remember, in marriage to submit one to another.

Remember what the Lord Jesus has done for me.

Remember not to murmur or complain.

Remember to remember God in our suffering.

Remember to remember the landmarks and the stones, remember?

Remember, Christianity is hard at times. Be the example and pattern, no excuses.

Remember the most important thing is to remember.

Remember God's plan gives hope, and the process leads to the prize.

Remember that Christ is sufficient for slaying all giants.

Remember there is but one God, one mediator, Christ Jesus.

Remember the enemy will attack when we are grief stricken and exhausted.

Remember to get stirred up because of the cross, the cost, and the communion.

Remember to glorify God with your conversation, which is your life.

Remember the God of Heaven is the uncaused first cause and eternal. We on the other hand; our lives are a vapor. Make today count.

Remember it's the intent of the heart that is all important.

Remember doing it God's way is rewarding good with blessing and rewarding bad with punishment.

Remember, Christianity has a creator God. All other religions have God created by man.

Remember you belong to the Lord. You are not your own.

Remember, don't leave your first love, the God of Heaven.

Remember, the God of Heaven completely forgives. Therefore, we should forgive.

Remember our Ebenezer stone. Hitherto, (up until now) the Lord helped us. He has brought us through. Henceforth, (from this point on) just say yes to the Lord Jesus concerning everything.

Remember, All of this and Heaven too.

Remember, don't be slow to believe. Remember, His words.

Remember, be grounded in greatness of godliness. Remember the Church, the place of truth.

Remember, God says, Go further and do better.

Remember, be a Church that has faith that works and work that is worth remembering.

Remember, it can happen to me: Departing from the faith, being deceived; falling for the doctrine of the devil.

Remember, choose to believe. We serve the God of the impossible.

Remember the miracles God has already done.

Remember, give words of faith; give good Doctrine (truth). Receive godly exercise; believing in the living God will cost me.

Remember; keep focusing on the One who is in control, Christ Jesus.

Remember to get all the way right with God.

Remember, live in a biblical reality. Read your Bible and act on what you've read.

Remember, when in a storm, cast these four anchors of faith: Be of good cheer (choose to be cheerful), fear not (God is in control), believe God (What He has said, His Word), and wait for the day (See what God does; let Him handle it).

Remember, no excuses. The right attitude concerning my limitations, expectations, operations, qualifications, and applications won't hinder me from having a testimony worth imitating.

Remember, the flesh profits nothing. The flesh never satisfies, never justifies, never sanctifies, and never multiplies. Die to the flesh and live for Christ.

Remember, the greatest temptation is to be your own God, to be separated from the one true God. We need the Bible, we need a watchman, and we need to worship God.

Remember, don't think it's evil to serve the Lord. Give it all to the Lord Jesus.

Remember to refuse, recuse, and retreat yourself from sin. Remember your position. You belong to Christ.

Remember, the God of Heaven is able to do it. We just need to give our all to it.

Remember, today is the day of salvation. We are all a heartbeat away from Heaven or Hell.

Remember, act as ladies and gentlemen. Be respectful of fathers, mothers, sisters, and brothers.

Remember, He is God alone in the storms (good times and bad). Through tests, trials, and temptation, ask for wisdom and believe God.

Remember, give a sacrifice of praise when suffering a lost. Praise God Anyway (PGA).

Remember, the Lord God of Heaven brought us this far and is the giver of all good things. Don't forget.

Remember, our High Priest is our very present help at, and in, all times.

Remember to confess all sin. Commit all things and commune always with Christ.

Remember, don't rely on self. There are only two options on the shelf, pleasing God or pleasing self. Help me Lord to stand for you at all times.

Remember to journey to Jericho where the Lord Jesus came to seek and save (you and me) the lost.

Remember, the evil one is coming after the King's kids.

Remember, sin had left a crimson stain. He washed it white as snow.

Remember; keep a zeal for the complete and perfect will of God.

Remember, it takes two mountains to make a valley. Amen and Amen.

Remember, priorities are important. Put the things of God first. Cultivate good soil by rightly managing the other things in your Christian life.

Remember, lay aside every weight. Don't live otherwise.

Remember, no matter what direction you go in this life, you will end up in front on the Lord Jesus someday.

Remember, we are just sinners saved by grace.

Remember, the little choices matter. Christ Jesus is worthy because of what He has done.

Remember, real success is found through godliness. Holiness with contentment is great gain.

Remember, abound in GRACE (God's riches at Christ's expense). Salvation bestows upon us the grace to give liberally to the work of God.

Remember, be prepared and be limitless in your willingness to give. Be responsible, represent Him well, and be ready for the Lord's return.

Remember, don't be entangled with the affairs of this life; it's leprosy. (Beware of attractions, and distractions. They get our attention, affection and determine our direction).

Remember, the devil is a liar. He is after our children. We need help, Lord; via prayer and fasting.

Remember, everyone will be without excuse. Salvation will be offered to all. Get saved and then get separated.

Remember, don't have the mindset of Sodom. Shame the devil. Be positive. Don't be satisfied with a sin and have a questioning, critical, complacent mindset. He died for you, live for Him.

Remember, be thankful for God's blessings, especially for a godly heritage.

Remember, be ye saved or lost, don't be an enemy of the cross. He loves you; be ye reconciled to God.

Remember, it's either money or the Master. With God all things are possible.

Remember, at salvation we have peace with God. We have access, we rejoice in hope, and we are reconciled and have joy.

Remember, being Christ-like is being more like Him and less like me. Have faith in God. Put off some things, put away some things, and replace them with godly things.

Remember, or be remembered negatively. Remember Lot's wife; don't look back longing for forbidden things. It breaks fellowship and gives place to the world, the flesh, and the devil.

Remember, look; behold the Lamb of God and know He is the Savior of the world. He alone can create life.

Remember, sanctification of home and family is important. No one can pray for your loved ones like you can. Through salvation I'm justi-fied: just as if I've never sinned.

Remember, your pastor is your star, over you shining the light of God's Word. Wise men still follow Him and his pastor today. They follow the pastor who leads them to the Master.

Remember, praise God that anyone can enter in at the straight gate. Pray, repent, and come to Christ today.

Remember, the evil one (Satan) wants you to fear. Be a witness. Fight against Satan and self. The Holy One wants you to reach the lost today.

Remember, when trouble comes; believe God, believe that 'It Is Well', and RUN to the man of God. God has given you a man of God to intercede for you.

Remember, beware. You may be on the narrow road but not in the middle of the road.

Remember, faith is belief in and, leaning on, the Lord Jesus no matter what, right now.

Remember, Christ says: "Remember Me." Partaking in the Lord's table is to be done in order to honor God, and being obedient and unified in doctrine and worship. Christ Jesus paid it all. Have a surrendered, submissive, and sanctified mind. Obey every authority, speak no evil of others, and be gentle. Therefore, being saved; glorify God.

Remember, the Lord Jesus Christ, the King of Kings, Lord of Lords has given us a full charge (praise, preach, go, give) to keep until He comes. He has all power.

Remember, a crisis of faith will come. Don't back up. Trust and obey. His grace is sufficient.

Remember, the Heavens of Heavens cannot contain Him. How is it that little man thinks he can explain Him? He is writing the story, and He has a greater ending.

Remember Jesus Christ. He is the same yesterday, today, and forever.

Remember to take heed; Pay attention. When the Lord Jesus speaks, His words are always, always right. They are spirit and life.

Remember, you have to get old, but you don't have to get ugly. A way not to get old is don't be born or die young.

Remember, we are part of something big, strong, and secure. Cast all your cares upon Him. Christ Jesus is God alone.

Remember, the 'in a minute' (imminent) return of Christ and live accordingly. Listen for the trumpet.

Remember, the God of Heaven is interested in your heart, head, and health. Trust and rejoice in the Lord always.

Remember, make headlines in Hell. Your enemy is real. Pick a side, witness, stand, pray, and obey.

Remember; order in the Church requires the servant of God standing for the truth of God, with the love of God, by the grace of God, and saved by God, for the Glory of God.

Remember, in the beginning God took nothing and made everything.

Remember, wait for it. Change will happen, and the final change is appointed.

Remember, if you understand why or not, trust, obey, go, find, follow, and say.

Remember, watch and pray.

Remember, the answer to prayer is: Nevertheless; thy will be done.

We will have trials, so remember the Lord Jesus has overcome the world.

He wants to share His victory with you; He is more interested in our Holiness than our happiness.

Remember, you don't have a soul; you are a soul, you have a body: Glorify God.

Remember, magnify His work. Make it the priority. It is what others behold.

Remember where you came from. Be joyful because He loved us; We love Him.

Remember, don't worry about tomorrow or fret about yesterday, and waste today.

Remember, your life should declare it because you say: Jesus Christ is King.

Remember, sometimes it is best to study to be silent.

Remember; Christ Jesus was forsaken, for my sake.

Remember, you have an identity, an influence, and an inheritance in your local Church by the grace, mercy, and peace of God.

Remember, your environment does not determine your destiny. God can use any man, Amen.

Remember, God has a purpose for my life.

Remember, the King James Bible is God's Word: Verbally inspired (God breathed), and preserved (kept forever). Be dedicated to reading it, obeying it, spreading it, and defending it.

Remember, go where you have been and somewhere you have never been and preach the gospel.

Remember, it is important to have a genuine walk with God. You are never alone. He has never forsaken you. See the need and take the lead.

Remember; don't keep Him locked out of His own. You belong to God. Reject idols, seek first Christ Jesus.

Remember when the Lord Jesus was your first love?

Remember, be diligent. Don't be slothful. Hard workers are winners.

Remember the faithful Word, the order in the Church. Problems in the church are people problems. Order requires us to stop it to avoid damaging whole houses. Rebuke deceivers and dividers sharply to keep things pure.

Remember, have conversations that are parallel with sound doctrine.

Remember, listening to God requires attention, reverence and obedience.

Remember, we cannot save anyone, but we are called to tell everybody, about Somebody who can save anybody.

Remember, choices matter. Is it morally, ethically and spiritually right? Make decisions according to God's Word.

Remember your zeal, your first love, your Lord and Savior Jesus Christ.

Remember, hold on to the things of God. If not, there are things you will throw away like faith, family, friends, finances, and future. God help us.

Thanksgiving: Thank you, Lord Jesus. "To the end that my glory may sing praise to thee, and not be silent. O Lord my God, I will give thanks unto thee for ever" (Psalm 30:12).

Remember, the worst thing to have is a headless woman and a heartless man. Husbands and wives lift each other up.

Remember, you represent Christ Jesus in a foreign country. Deliver the message of hope with a meek and humble attitude.

Remember, have the right position and disposition.

Remember; get all the way right with God, no matter the price.

Remember; cast all recognition, awards, and crowns to Him. He is worthy. Praise the Lord. Trust God in difficult times. He will direct your paths, therefore, follow Jesus Christ.

Remember Christmas at Calvary. Christ died to redeem whosoever will.

Remember, even in the great tribulation, God's grace is greater.

Remember; that where God guides, He provides the perfect will of God, which is the safest place to be.

Remember, you are laying up treasure in Heaven for His sake.

Remember we, the saved, are without excuse. Witness to the lost.

Remember; what the God of Heaven wants for Christmas is you.

Remember; walk in the light you are given. Immediately obey the scriptures and worship the Savior, surrendering all.

Remember; not only is nothing impossible with God but when put in His hands, the impossible is probable.

Remember, they are the Ten Commandments, not the ten suggestions.

Remember, don't just sit on the premises, but stand on His promises. Fight the world, the flesh and the devil. Finish well.

"When I remember these things, I pour out my soul in me: for I had gone with the multitude, I went with them to the house of God, with the voice of joy and praise, with a multitude that kept holyday" (Psalm 42:4).

God loves you. He desires a personal relationship with you that is real. He wants to be your Savior and your friend.

Chapter 19

Sexual Harassment, SD Card, SOS, Surrender, Salvation, Servanthood, sSs, STDs, Songs,

Save our Souls, Sick of Sin, Slave of Sin, Stuck on Stupid, Sin, Satan, and Self

"I Took Your V Card and You Liked It, Kentucky Woman Allegedly Raped 12-Year-Old Boy, Made Him and His Friends Call Her Mom."[83]

What does it say for our culture when women start being accused of this wicked behavior?

Sexual harassment claims put a new meaning to the phrase, "Draining the swamp." Be it morning, noon, or the middle of the night, eventually the truth will come to the light.

"Be not deceived; God is not mocked: for whatsoever a man soweth, that shall he also reap" (Galatians 6:7).

Well, I couldn't help but respond to the many harassment claims addressed in the media; Allegations against President Trump, Johnny Anderson, Joe Barton, Mario Batali, John Besh, Eric Bolling, Louis C. K., Nick Carter, Bill Clinton, John Conyers, Keith Ellison, Blake Farenthold, Al Franken, Morgan Freeman, Eric Greitens, Mark Halperin, Bill Hybels, Garrison Keillor, Ruben Kihuan, Matt Lauer, James Levin, Cardinal Theodore Edgar McCarrick, Melanie Martinez, Les Moonves,

Roy Moore, Larry Nasser, Bill O'Reilly, Brett Ratner, Jerry Richardson, Charlie Rose, Eric Schneiderman, Kevin Spacey, Russell Simmons, Travis Smiley, David Sweeney, Jeffery Tambor, Glenn Thrush, Harvey Weinstein, and Gregg Zaun etc.

Could it be that "draining the swamp" is providential; The Divine revealing the sins of men? What does your worldview provide as a solution for the darkness of sexual harassment and assault in the past, present, and future?

Now, the GOoD news (God's Good News): The Christian, King James biblical worldview is that this is nothing new. It's the Same Old Sin (SOS), but a different day. No sin goes unseen, or unpunished (Galatians 6:7–8). There are zero unsolved crimes because payday is coming someday in this life or in the next (Romans 2:6–11).

That said, the solution to sexual harassment and assault is building godly character in young people. For instance, we are encouraged to give our twelve year olds shots to prevent Human Papilloma Virus (HPV); but why not teach them (boys and girls alike) to avoid intimacy until marriage and to respect others? This includes teaching them to speak up when mistreated to stop predators from abusing additional victims. You see, biblical character is all about others (Philippians 2:3–11). Biblical character produces right decision making at an early age (Proverbs 22:6).

What about older offenders? We need a culture that is God centered, one that promotes righteous living and judgment that is accompanied by timely administered justice. This means innocent until proven guilty and punishment when found guilty. Oh, wait a minute, this would mean rejecting our atheist-driven culture and embracing one nation under God (Titus 3:1–8), yes indeed.

Consider Christ ANEW, nothing else will do (Ecclesiastes 12:13–14).

Say What?

"STD cases hit record high in US."[84]

A former slogan was, "Yes we can." I say, oh no you didn't! I had to laugh to keep from crying when the National News report ended with this comment; "some say the rise in STDs are due to the increased popularity of dating apps." Really, I wonder if our former President, Barack Obama, would evolve to support this, aforementioned, position.

That said, now the GOoD news (God's Good News): Who or what is to blame for the rising STD numbers? The Christian, King James biblical worldview is that all imperfection is due to the fall of mankind (i.e., original sin). In this case, our immoral behavior is to blame (1 Corinthians 6:9–10). The sin of mankind is the culprit (Proverbs 16:25).

You see, we don't get to change God's design for intimacy without consequences. Again, God's design for intimacy in humans is one man and one woman for one lifetime in the marriage relationship (Genesis 2:21–24). Anything else is sin, confusion, and the major cause of STDs. God's plan for intimacy and everything else is always best. God loves us all and desires a personal relationship with us that is real. Coming to Him on His terms, and then living His way is the key to abundant life (Romans 10:9–13). What does your worldview give as the cause for the rise in STDs? And does your worldview provide a solution? Consider Christ ANEW. He is the solution too (John 10:10).

I really enjoy godly songs, and there are two things that are akin to angel's wings: The sound of the choir when only women sing, and the sound of turning pages of scripture, right before the sermon the Pastor brings. To date, here are some of my favorite songs:

- Above All
- A Sinner Like Me
- All I Ever Want to Be
- God's Been Good
- Heart of Praise
- In Christ Alone
- I've Been Blessed
- Jesus What A Saviour
- Treasured (A Patch the Pirate rendition)

God loves you. He desires a personal relationship with you that is real. He wants to be your Savior and your friend.

I'll fly away
BMk 2018

Chapter 20

The Truth, You Can Trust it, Twitter, Two kinds of Slavery (Racism Revisited)

TWO KINDS OF modern day slavery:
1) Being a slave to the sin of unforgiveness
2) Being a slave to sin by rejecting Christ Jesus as your personal Lord and Savior (the only unforgivable sin)

Here is the prelude to the answer to racism; Total forgiveness. No longer be a slave; become a son by finding your purpose, self-worth, and fulfillment in the man, Christ Jesus.

The goal: A generation that unconditionally forgives.

We suffer when we don't know, or accept, that we live in a sin cursed world.

Injustice does exist and should be called out but, there is no defense for love.

"Black High School Quarterback Ejected After Complaining to Ref About Opponent Calling Him a Racial Slur."[85]

"Black woman accused of posing as white Ku Klux Klan member to threaten neighbors faces terrorist charges."[86]

"Sen. Coleman Young II Speaks out against racial injustice."[87]

Having a dream versus living the dream

This was passed to me with the caption, "very powerful." Well, with all due respect to the Senator, time will tell how powerful. If it is helpful, the speech will be remembered for not condoning any sin while encouraging everyone to value others. The "I have a Dream" speech was given on August 28, 1963, and yet here we are today—still dreaming. Dreaming is okay, but "People who look like us;" a phrase often used by minorities, need to wake up and start demonstrating moral character that brings about praiseworthy recognition. How?

Now, the GOoD news (God's Good News): the Christian, King James biblical worldview is that value isn't determined by acceptance or nationality. All lives have equal value and matter because they're God given. Pursuing a life that glorifies God is the answer to racism (Proverbs 3:1–6).

A personal relationship with Jesus Christ, who is no respecter of persons, unites us (Galatians 3:26–28). You see, because He loves me, I will love you even if you hate me (Romans 12:17–21). Again, the sin of our day is unforgiveness (John 8:34–36). My desire for you and your loved ones is abundant life now and, a heavenly home someday. Trusting in Christ frees us from the cares of this world (Philippians 1:21). Life with contentment is great gain.

Conclusion: At least fifty-four years of dreaming, sleep walking, and talking, It's high-time we start living by unconditionally loving and forgiving one another (Ephesians 4:31–32). Ultimately, it's not where you've been, it's where you're going (1 Peter 4:7–11).

What does your worldview give as the solution for racial injustice? Consider Christ ANEW (Absolutely Nothing Else Works).

TWEETS

Time is short, so are tweets; I joined the Twitter craze for a time but since I purposed in my heart not to be a slave to anything but the cause of Christ; I curtailed my tweeting and will only do so if spiritually lead.

I initially hated the idea of "tweeting" as it appears to be a way of venting without explaining the rationale for one's rant. Below are some of my, personal, tweets:

God Bless America when we CONSIDER ... "All gave some, some gave all"; but only One died for the enemy, CHRIST. Luke 23:33-43; Romans 5:6-8

You know you're OLD when: You find yourself on the verge of celebrating; WooHoo! 280 Twitter characters! and Whaat? Y2K Babies graduating?

Works Proverb: Seeing The New Jerusalem; unloading hay, stubble, wood: Being Heavenly minded, earthly good. Consider Christ. James 2:14-20

Yet another great Lord's day. So blessed to hear HIM, through our Pastor, say: "Consider Christ! and Follow Me; TODAY!" Hebrews 12

In this climate of dread; God hath said: "We will be ALIVE; a lot longer than we are dead." John: 5:24 Consider Christ ANEW; He loves you.

Train up a child in the way he should go, and point him to The Saviour we want him to know. Consider Christ

Happy birthday Sharon Lundin; this prayer is for me: Help me Lord to remember others, the way you remembered me. Consider Christ. Romans 5:6

Faith Baptist, revival: So thankful I am in my place, Jesus in the midst; me a beggar blessed to witness one saved by grace...

THERE AIN'T NOTHING GREATER THAN GRACE!!! Ephesians 2:4-10

Tks first responders! Honored to share this day; but envious of your toys as Grandfathers are Antique Little Boys... Proverbs 16:31

Happy First Responders and National Grandparents Day. Consider Christ ANEW (Absolutely Nothing Else Works). Romans 13:7

'Irma' praying for all effected by hurricanes; and Family in Miami, Quincy, Atlanta and Faith Baptist Church, Walterboro SC. Romans 8:38-39

Irma-geddon? Just another reason to pray everyday, in a world cursed by sin. Consider Christ ANEW, He loves you. John 16:33; John 3:8

Kudos to POTUS for the NatDP; but we can't stop now, continue to Labor, everyday for him and our nation. PRAY!!! 1 Thessalonians 5:17; James 5:16

Corona Mass Ejection: What happens when a "Baptist" gets saved and sees "The Wedding Ring." 2 Corinthians 5:17; 2 Corinthians 6:17-18

Darkness to light, 21 August: Couldn't help but recall 21 November 1999, I gave my life to Christ. Bless His Holy Name. John 8:12

Angel Wings: The choir when only the women sing; the sound pages of God's Word makes right before the message our Pastor brings. 1 John 1:5-7, Psalm 40:3

Eclipse this (pun intended): Blessed to have all 3 grandchildren under my roof today. Consider Christ ANEW. He is so good. Psalm 127: 1-5

NAT. Lefty Day: If the left side of the brain controls the right hand; then only left-handed people are in their right minds. Judges 20:16

Coming off another great Lord's day; my prayer for all is that we glorify Him in everything we think, do and say. Consider Christ 1 Cor 2:9

Just viewed the Wed, 2 Aug, FBC service via vimeo. The mystery isn't the coming eclipse; it is that He uses the least of us. Eph. 3:7-12

A little late to reply but, «monkeys and the evolutionary theory" come to mind when I hear/see the word primate.

Praying for our nation; may our leaders, at least, play nice. Our hope is in The One who paid the greatest price. Consider Christ. Prov. 29:2

Wow! So thankful you are ok; He (The God of Heaven) does do all things well.

Thankful: Another great Lord's day. He's worthy worship for all He'll do. Consider Christ ANEW (Absolutely Nothing Else Works). Psalm 111:1

Hey yall', a shout out to Faith Baptist, Walterboro SC: When a little girl says "Thank God for the work, I love my room." IT WAS WORTH IT ALL!!

NBT's awesome. It ain't over, we've got one more night. The Lord "Jesus is The Light." Consider Christ. He is always, always right. John 8:12

Patients Prayer: Lord, grant me the patients to LOVE as you love me, COURAGE to show it openly, TESTIMONY to make a difference 2 Thess 3:5.

Division litmus test? A quote attr. to W. Penn says it best: "Men must be governed by God or they will be ruled by tyrants" Prov. 29:2.

Done napping: Worked a little too hard today but blessed I could serve this week; getting older reminds me, my flesh is weak. Matthew 23:41

Blessed: Beyond measure; so much so I could burst. "If I knew grandchildren were so wonderful I would have had them first." Psalm 127:3-5

Feeling unnoticed? For the things of God you thirst? Fear not, the Word of God always recognizes the rejected lines first. Matthew 19:29-30

Idols of a Godless world; from these 3 flee: Strong drink, corrupt communication, ungodly intimacy. Proverbs 20:1, Psalm 59:12, Proverbs 5

Thankful: Salvation is for any, not just some; Perfect love manifested in: Whosoever will, can come. Consider Christ. Psalm 18:30, Acts 4:12

Praying: Whether near Aiken, Fayetteville or Punxsutawney; keep us safe Lord. We are one in Christ Jesus: Family ... Go ISC!!! 2 Cor. 2:14

Amazed: I'm kept throughout the night, forgiven and given a fresh start come morning light. Consider Christ ANEW; He loves you. Psalm 51:10

Congrats students, staff and parents of Faith Baptist Academy. Your faithfulness and hard work gives hope to folks like me. Proverbs 22:6

Thankful for another day, and a special occasion to convey: The crowd may be going the wrong way; what does The KJ Bible say? Hebrews 4:12

*LGBT: God said it; that settles it. If you or I believe it, or not: *Let God Be True. Consider Christ ANEW. Gen 2:18-25; Rom 1:18-27

*TGIF: Thank God for another day; this a Sabbath letter; For His grace and mercy? *Thank God Its Forever. Consider Christ. 2 Thess. 2:16-17

*PGA: Praising God in sickness or health. Heirs with Christ, eternal wealth. Abundant life everyday; today? Chick-fil-A *Praise God Anyway

Rejoicing in a great week in Christ Jesus so pardon my tribal, Salkehatchie, yell: HE HATH DONE ALL THINGS WELL!!!!!!!!! Psalm 146:1-10

Praying: Rice Festival outreach; Lord as we provide the feet; be glorified as You provide the heat and Living Water that's meet. John 7:38

Amazed: The God of Heaven fixed a small thing this morn, I thought "that's odd?" Then this came to mind; "What's big to God"? Rev 1:8

Apostasy, Moral decay, Political anarchy? We continue to slip? Fear not, Christ is coming: Righteous Dictatorship. Consider Him, Psalm 9:6-9

Actually it matters how straight the gate; The broad road you roll? I'll take the straight and narrow and save my soul. Matthew 7:13-14

Considering all my blessings under the Son; it's awesome to see all that is being done. Consider Christ ANEW. He loves you. Ephesians 1:1-6

Why 4 Gospels? Good News to the prophetic, powerful, perfect seeking, poverty stricken: Behold, The Man Christ Jesus quickens. Eph 2:1-10

What an April! A giraffe is born and standing, witnesses tell. All creation is redeemed: He is risen! Jesus is alive and well. 1 Cor 15:1-8

The real *MOAB? Ruth; From Obed through David on to The Truth. (* Mother Of All Balm) Consider Christ ANEW. Jeremiah 17:14, Revelation 22:2

Goal: Live on a high level; wear the full armor of God to combat that Evil trinity: The World, Flesh and Devil. Consider Christ. Eph 6:10-20

Praying for a prayer life of fruit, bountiful; To avoid Lisa Simpson's critique: "Prayer, the last desperate act of a scoundrel" Matt 6:9-13

Awoke to Heaven reflecting The Son; The moon, and stars, fully shows He has done: Resurrection! Jesus is Light. Genesis 1:1-4, John 8:12

Having crazy dreams: Why and what are they all about? Remembered a gov't saying: Garbage in, garbage out. Consider Christ ANEW Proverbs 4:23

5 "life" languages? Faith, Hope, Love is within reach; A personal relationship with Him, Joy and Peace. Consider Christ ANEW. 1 Cor 13:12-13

"Blue Zones; places where people forget to die" CNN letter. Live 121 yrs? Good. Abundant, eternal life: Better. Consider Christ. Heb 9:27-28

Storms in the forecast? The safe place to be is having your hand in The Hand of The Man who calmed the sea. Consider Christ. Nahum 1:3

Oh the exceeding sinfulness of sin: 1 John 1:9 comes to mind; repent, start all over again. S.O.S. (Sick Of Sin); Consider Christ. Rom 5:19-21

Smiling at 128,679 folks watching April, the giraffe. A multitude will see The Lamb one day; that truth has made me laugh. Revelation 7:9-12

Glorious Tuesday! Similar to every day in The New Jerusalem: Worship and song, Consider Christ and "Bow The Knee" all day long. Psalm 98:4

Praying with/for the youth & staff at The Wilds RSC. Praising God, in advance, for what He will do this week. Psalm 150 @CarolinasRSC

In the mirror, what do I see? Failure to walk "Circumspectly." Sorry; inside joke for my church family. Consider Christ. Ephesians 5:15-16

Separation of Church and State: Depending on mankind for "Progress?" Reaping the opposite are we? Congress. Consider Christ. Psalm 118:8

Blessed by, my friends, the men of Faith Baptist Church, Walterboro, SC. Ladies, the pizza was good!! Consider Christ. Proverbs 27:17; 18:24

Legal Marijuana: criminal incentive less? Denver & all, want perks? Consider Christ ANEW (Absolutely Nothing Else Works) Rom 14:22; Matt 6:33

Fear someone (FBI, CIA, NSA etc.) is watching you? Let's glorify God in all we think, say, or do. Consider Christ ANEW. Ecclesiastes12:13-14

Anxious about a stalled travel ban? The homeland is safe and secure in The Masters hand. Consider Christ ANEW, He loves you Romans 8:38-39

Simple minded? The missing link (ttb.org). High IQ? Let my people think (rzim.org). Consider HIM. Matt 11:28-30

Please pray for Compassion International, the nation of India, and our *GFI son Vishnu. Consider Christ, Proverbs 14:34 *Grand Fathered In

Still giddy since The Lords day so while walking in that way; you may see me before a mirror utter, "What does The Bible say?" Hebrews 12:2

Happy birthday to my "grand" son Benjamin; 3 yrs old today, the son of my right hand. To all sons: Consider Christ–Proverbs 10:1

Yes! Pres honors USN Seal Owens. "All gave some, some gave all" but, only One died for the enemy, Christ Jesus. Consider Him–Romans 5:8-10

Great Lords day (26 Feb) followed by "floods" of fellowship at Faith Baptist Church, Walterboro, SC. Philippians 4:4-9 ...so ...

Hooray for Holy-Wood!! The Oscar goes to "The Cross." Consider Christ; in a sin cursed world He is "the only chance we've got." 2 Cor. 5:21

Wow! CNN & Pres Trump get it right? CNN reports: "SWEDEN: Riots erupt in Stockholm" immigrant "neighborhood." Consider Christ, Romans 13:7

A belated Happy Valentine's to my wife: You're God's gift to me; I love you. Proverbs 18:22…

Praying for our nation and lonely souls this V-day week-end: Heads up, Look up, and Consider Christ. Proverbs 14:34; Philippians 2:5-11

"I hope you don't mind" if I improve this song: "How wonderful life is", Christ Jesus came in the world! Consider Christ, 1 Timothy 1:15

Thank God for the ministries of Faith Baptist Church, Walterboro SC; Any man can be a New Man. Consider Christ; Colossians 3:10-11

Are we all really a nation of immigrants? Yes, the God of Heaven owns it all... Genesis 1:1; 1 Timothy 6:7

...Because immigrants that look like you and me want to commit terror, enter illegally etc., we need restraint...–Proverbs 14:34

...this means you and I may be detained. Wait a minute! The good sacrificing for the bad? Consider Christ–1 Peter 3:18

@Pastor Tony Jones Thank you Faith Baptist Church for praying for us and being a friend. Consider Christ–Proverbs 18:24

A lot of fuss over executive orders; in a sin cursed world: In God we trust, all others we monitor. Consider Christ ANEW*, He loves you......*
Absolutely Nothing Else Works

i don't need 4LTE power, i don't need 3G. as i sojourn today, *2G is enough for me. as i travel this sod, my desire is to *Glorify God.

Happy Birthday Alexander J Mueller born @ 6:56am today and his uncle Eric J Moss, born on this day in 1970. To all: Consider Christ ANEW!

So thankful for another day; this glorious Christmas morn, especially when your chiefest thought is: Merry Christmas, Christ is born! Isaiah 9:6

God loves you. He desires a personal relationship with you that is real. He wants to be your Savior and your friend.

HOME IS WHERE THE "BORDER" IS.

MATTHEW 7:13-14

BHM 2018

Chapter 21

Ugly Unbelief: The Root of Evil, Violence, and Spiritual Heart Issues

"The Black church is having a moment."[88]

THIS HEADLINE ITSELF exposes the ungodly, so called church. There is no such thing as "the Black" church in genuine Christianity. One must be rooted in unbelief to ignore or disavow this:

"There is neither Jew nor Greek, there is neither bond nor free, there is neither male nor female: for ye are all one in Christ Jesus" (Galatians 3:28).

The church is not defined by race or denominations. Anyone who believes the Gospel, sincerely repents, and turns their sinful life over to Jesus Christ is forgiven and placed in the Church. Until an individual is genuinely born again, he or she can never appreciate the whole counsel of God (1 Corinthians 15:3–4). Real Christians believe their King James Bible from cover to cover. We even believe the cover: *The Holy Bible*.

Unbelief is ugly. Remember the saying, "You have to get old but you don't have to get ugly?" Well, aging and being discontented is rooted in unbelief. Here's a helpful acronym: UGLY (Unconditionally, God Loves You). Trusting and resting in Christ Jesus allows us to finish well.

Re-visiting COVID-19
Protests and what unbelief produces from the hardened heart.

"New models released by the White House on Tuesday show that 100,000 to 240,000 people could die in the U.S. from Coronavirus, even with most Americans staying home…We don't accept that number. We're going to do everything we can to get that number even below that," Dr. Anthony Fauci said at the White House's daily coronavirus briefing.

What if the God of Heaven is using this to show us something? What if COVID-19 is God's tool, squeezing mankind's heart, to reveal what's already in it. We need a Savior.

"The heart is deceitful above all things, and desperately wicked: who can know it?" (Jeremiah 17:9).

Now, the GOoD news (God's Good News): Christ Jesus saves and changes hearts. Change the heart of the man and you change where he makes a stand. Hope is available to all that put their trust in Him. With Christ, "No end in sight" takes on new meaning—everlasting life. This changes everything as physical life, with contentment, is great gain.

Christ alone is the answer for whatever ails us, be it systemic or pandemic, all imperfection is the result of living in a sin-cursed world.

Why not lay on your pillow tonight with the peace that passes all understanding. Again, genuine Christians are the silent majority. "One, with God is the majority"- Martin Luther. Genuine Christians are not protesting anything, we are promoting Christ Jesus. Consider Christ ANEW, He loves you.

He is pleading, "Come unto me, all ye that labour and are heavy laden, and I will give you rest. Take my yoke upon you, and learn of me; for I am meek and lowly in heart: and ye shall find rest unto your souls. For my yoke is easy, and my burden is light" (Matthew 11:28–30).

Regrets

If I had to make a list of regrets; the greatest would be not coming to Christ at a younger age. That said, my pastor settled that one for me when he said, "You will be dead far longer than you will be alive;" that brings to mind one of my favorite sayings: Life is Good but, Eternal Life if Better. I'm so thankful for my *One Sincere Moment*. I was born on the July 4th, 1959; but born again on November 21st, 1999, praise the Lord.

God loves you. He desires a personal relationship with you that is real. He wants to be your Savior and your friend.

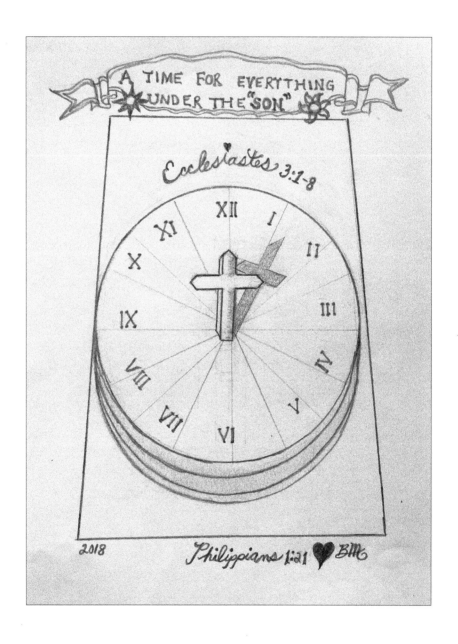

Chapter 22

Victory in Christ and Voting

WHICH WAY ARE you going to vote?

"Biden ally suggests Iowa caucus process more restrictive than Texas voting law."[89]

Why would someone want Iowa out as the first state for voting, too conservative?

"Trump infuriated after backing Alabama loser."[90]

"Biden defeats Trump in an election he made about character of the nation and the President."[91]

This is quite entertaining as it gives us an opportunity to examine ourselves. Are we infuriated when we back a loser?

Now, the GOoD news (God's Good News): Christians, those who give their lives to Christ, hold the King James biblical worldview. We have a sure foundation to use when deciding who to back or vote for. I support candidates whose lifestyle, conduct, character, stump speeches, voting record, political affiliation, and everything he or she stands for agrees the most with the God of Heaven, Christ Jesus. His stance on the issues is given to us through the Bible.

Therefore, considering every issue from A to Z; from abortion to the death penalty, the economy, homosexuality, marriage, to Zion and beyond; It doesn't matter if you are black, white, red or blue; you agree with the God of Heaven and I'll vote for you (Psalm 118:8).

Why he or she that agrees the most? Because God's ways are perfect; none of us would qualify as a perfect candidate (Isaiah 53:6); and yes, I will vote because I'm to be in the world but not like it (Mathew 5:16). Therefore, we encourage all to consider Christ (Matthew 11:28–30).

The really good news is that true Christians can sleep peacefully on election night, after voting righteously; they know God is still in control (Proverbs 21:1). What does your worldview give as a method for choosing the best candidate?

Did America choose wisely in the last election, or should they have sided with the previous President? Time and consequences will tell. It all comes down to your personal worldview. Is it trustworthy?

God loves you. He desires a personal relationship with you that is real. He wants to be your Savior and your friend.

Chapter 23

Wars, Works and Worldviews, Who, What, Where, Why, When. Wait for It

"The Marxist Underpinnings of BLM Organizations."[92]

OUR PERSONAL WORLDVIEW is very important, it is the foundation for why we believe, what we believe: What, Why, Where (WWW). Is your worldview grounded in the world wide web of the internet? Have you done enough to please God? The difference between "Do" and "Done" is what separates true Christianity from every other religion, philosophy, atheistic, agnostic, and common-sense idea that has ever been suggested or imagined. Again, the key is comparison. While everything else says do this or that, Christ Jesus said, "It is finished," done (John 19:30).

What does your worldview offer that answers life and death questions? What do you believe, why do you believe it, and where did you get that belief system from? See ISOAR in chapter 9. We need solutions, time is running out.

"Weathering the 'One day at a time': Bahamians displaced by Dorian seek solace in South Florida."[93]

I prayed for those in the Bahamas and everyone who had been impacted by hurricane Dorian. During the storm, as it started to move, after being stagnant over the Bahamas; this came to mind: Dorian's behavior is akin to our lives if we are not careful. Like an unresponsive yoyo toy, it just sat there spinning, not moving forward. So is life apart from God. When doing our own thing, we can be oblivious of the world around us, and yet leave a path of destruction. Yes, we may not be responsible for how bad things are, but will things be better after we leave the scene? "And as it is appointed unto men once to die, but after this the judgment" (Hebrews 9:27).

We all need a solid foundation for what is right and wrong. We need the God of Heaven, Christ Jesus.

"The Lord is slow to anger, and great in power, and will not at all acquit the wicked: the Lord hath his way in the whirlwind and in the storm, and the clouds are the dust of his feet" (Nahum 1:3). Consider Christ ANEW (Absolutely Nothing Else Works) and know your purpose for being here too. "Let your light so shine before men, that they may see your good works, and glorify your Father which is in heaven" (Matthew 5:16).

"Russia launches full-scale attack in Ukraine, dozens dead."[94]

"Every purpose is established by counsel: and with good advice make war" (Proverbs 20:18).

"Biden says he's now convinced Putin has decided to invade Ukraine, but leaves door open for diplomacy."[95]

"And ye shall hear of wars and rumours of wars: see that ye be not troubled: for all these things must come to pass, but the end is not yet" (Matthew 24:6).

As for wars, indeed time is running out. The God of Heaven is still in control. Trusting Him is all important.

God loves you. He desires a personal relationship with you that is real. He wants to be your Savior and your friend.

Chapter 24

Xtremist, Terrorist and Hardened Hearts, Xenophobia

"The Trump Doctrine: Terrorists Lose and Peace Wins."[96]

"Trump's racism and xenophobia haven't caught on."[97]

YES, I KNOW "Xtremist" is an incorrect spelling of extremist. I did this on purpose for a certain professor of religious studies that I will not name, but being a stickler for grammar, he missed the entire point. Here is a gist of his critique. He opined that a certain "Christian song" should not be desirable because, for rhyming sake, the English language was butchered. He is clearly, and extremely, ignorant of the Word of God. We "Christians," should be building up believers versus cutting them down. I wonder what the professor's favorite Christian song is? Therefore, a terrorist can come in many flavors and may very well be your professor.

That said, it brings me to the point of this section which is the hardened heart. As I mentioned before, when scripture talks of God hardening someone's heart it simply means He squeezes out what was inside it all along. Yes, we (mankind) are phony to the core. Yes, "The heart is deceitful above all things, and desperately wicked: who can know it?" (Jeremiah 17:9).

While we try to portray an acceptable appearance, God ensures that our true character is revealed. Thus, the reason In God we trust, all others we monitor.

Law and order and border security are not Xenophobia measures.

What does your worldview give for the solution to terrorism and border security?

Change the heart of the man and you change where he stands. Terrorism is yet another result of a sin-cursed world. "And this is the condemnation, that light is come into the world, and men loved darkness rather than light, because their deeds were evil" (John 3:19).

The good news is salvation in Christ alone is the solution and available to whosoever will. Will what? Die to self.

"For the wages of sin is death; but the gift of God is eternal life through Jesus Christ our Lord" (Romans 6:23).

God loves you. He desires a personal relationship with you that is real. He wants to be your Savior and your friend.

Chapter 25

Yo! Y'all, it is all about the Alcohol, Your Life Matters

"Alcohol Abuse Is on the Rise, but Doctors Too Often Fail to Treat it."[98]

HAVE YOU NOTICED the fascination that America, and the world, has with alcohol? The oracle of beer: six degrees of conversation; it's all about the beer. While it is true that we are six or fewer social connections away from a drunkard; it's rooted in the sin of greed which leads to destruction.

"Wine is a mocker, strong drink is raging: and whosoever is deceived thereby is not wise" (Proverbs 20:1).

Making drinking cool is profitable to some, but hurts everyone. "For the love of money is the root of all evil: which while some coveted after, they have erred from the faith, and pierced themselves through with many sorrows" (1 Timothy 6:10).

Yo, y'all, it's all about the alcohol. Want to be and stay cool? The good news: A young preacher, Isaiah Jones, said: Get Saved With Amazing Grace (SWAG) and really live. Being SWAG provides complete satisfaction.

"And be not drunk with wine, wherein is excess; but be filled with the Spirit" (Ephesians 5:18).

"ESPN President John Skipper resigns citing substance abuse issue."[99]

"Autopsy: Oklahoma State student died of alcohol poisoning."[100]

"Deaths from drug, alcohol overdoses skyrocket in Maryland."[101]

Again, have you noticed this world's fascination with alcohol? The sad bottom line is that we have fallen for the lie that drinking is cool. This, like a lot of evils, is rooted in the love of money. What does your worldview give as the reason for drug and alcohol abuse? Well pride, and peer pressure are causes for the heartache suffered due to substance abuse. We have a culture that glorifies drug and alcohol use. Oh, it is cool to get high or to be wasted.

Now, the GOoD news (God's Good News): The King James biblical worldview is that anyone who defiles the crown of God's creation, their body, is not wise (Proverbs 20:1). You see, the God of Heaven created everything else before creating mankind. This reveals two things:

First, because we created nothing, we don't own anything, including ourselves. We are merely stewards (James 1:17).

Secondly, as the crown of God's creation, the original plan was for mankind to have a special relationship with God (Genesis 1:27–28). This personal love relationship was ruined when Adam's sin of disobedience ushered in death; spiritually and physically (Romans 5:12). This disobedience continues today. We live in a selfish culture that glorifies bad, calling it good (Isaiah 5:20).The promotion of ungodly behavior is the result of a sin-cursed world.

The good news is that there is hope. Life can be worth living without any assistance from substances. Being saved with amazing grace (SWAG) is the remedy for a nation or individual seeking a reason to live (Matthew 11:28). Knowing who God is and how special we are gives us a purpose for being here (John 10:10). Consider Christ ANEW. He offers the spiritual high; nothing else will satisfy.

Again, your life matters (YLM). Have you ever considered yourself a miracle? To date, we have exceeded eight billion individuals on this planet and only one you. God loves you. You are unique and wonderfully made. "I will praise thee; for I am fearfully and wonderfully made: marvellous are thy works; and that my soul knoweth right well" (Psalm 139:14).

When possible, Google the World Population Clock and watch the births tick away. Then consider that each one is unique from any other person who has ever been born, miraculous! You are a miracle. Being created in His image ensures your uniqueness (Isaiah 45:18).

God desires a personal relationship with you that is real. He wants to be your Savior and your friend.

Chapter 26

Zion: Still God's Chosen, He is Not Done with Israel Yet, The Remnant and Remembering

"Israeli court ruling on major holy site angers Palestinians."[102]

"Israel's election ended with neither a Netanyahu-led bloc nor an alliance of his opponents winning a majority."[103]

IN CONCLUSION, I'D be remiss not mention God's chosen; the nation Israel. God is not done with them yet. Like them, you are loved and wanted presently in this sin-cursed world. The nation of Israel will have no peace until they return, spiritually, to the land (Ezekiel 37:21–25).

Yes, they are back in the land but not as, biblically, prophesied. When they fully return, their hearts will be changed. Also, like them, you must repent and believe the Gospel to be eternally in His presence. You must be born again. Our sin separates us from God. The God of Heaven cannot coexist with imperfection, therefore we must repent.

To repent means to change your mind, to turn away from your way of doing things. When doing so, you must turn to the one true God, Christ Jesus, the God of Abraham, Isaac, and Jacob.

The Gospel is "good news." Jesus Christ lived and died a sacrificial death so your sins could be forgiven. The Gospel is bad news for those who reject it. His resurrection ensures that physical death will not be the end for all who believe and put their trust in Him. The God of Heaven has provided redemption to all who come to Him by faith.

The God of heaven will completely return His chosen people to the land of Israel someday.

"But now thus saith the LORD that created thee, O Jacob, and he that formed thee, O Israel, Fear not: for I have redeemed thee, I have called thee by thy name; thou art mine. When thou passest through the waters, I will be with thee; and through the rivers, they shall not overflow thee: when thou walkest through the fire, thou shalt not be burned; neither shall the flame kindle upon thee. For I am the LORD thy God, the Holy One of Israel, thy Saviour: I gave Egypt for thy ransom, Ethiopia and Seba for thee. Since thou wast precious in my sight, thou hast been honourable, and I have loved thee: therefore will I give men for thee, and people for thy life. Fear not: for I am with thee: I will bring thy seed from the east, and gather thee from the west; I will say to the north, Give up; and to the south, Keep not back: bring my sons from far, and my daughters from the ends of the earth; Even every one that is called by my name: for I have created him for my glory, I have formed him; yea, I have made him"(Isaiah 43:1–7).

"For there is one God, and one mediator between God and men, the man Christ Jesus" (1 Timothy 2:5).

"And the Word was made flesh, and dwelt among us, (and we beheld his glory, the glory as of the only begotten of the Father,) full of grace and truth" (John 1:14).

"For I delivered unto you first of all that which I also received, how that Christ died for our sins according to the scriptures; And that he was buried, and that he rose again the third day according to the scriptures"(1 Corinthians 15:3–4).

"Let us hear the conclusion of the whole matter: Fear God, and keep his commandments: for this is the whole duty of man. For God shall bring every work into judgment, with every secret thing, whether it be good, or whether it be evil"(Ecclesiastes 12:13–14).

God loves you and He desires a personal relationship with you that is real. He wants to be you Savior and your friend.

Isaiah 11:6

"The wolf also shall dwell with the lamb, and the leopard shall lie down with the kid; and the calf and the young lion and the fatling together; and a little child shall lead them" (Isaiah 11:6).

The End is the beginning—life everlasting.

Endnotes

Chapter 1

1. Sam Dorman; Fox News, California parents request judge block public schools from asking students to pray to Aztec gods, Fox News, 29 September 202, Published September 29, 2021 10:39am EDT; https://www.foxnews.com/us/california-students-pray-aztec-gods-school-lawsuit

2. Are the Ten Commandments still relevant today? Oct. 30, 2017, Fox News Video; https://news.yahoo.com/ten-com-mandments-still-relevant-today-201904631.html

3. Logan Crews, The issue with Keep the Christ in Christmas: November 19, 2020, https://trinitonian.com/2020/11/19/the-issue-with-keep-the-christ-in-christmas/

4. Associated Press, House of Cards ending amid Kevin Spacey sexual harassment claim. Trump declares Opioid crisis a 'public health emergency, Published: 4:04 PM EDT October 30, 2017, Updated: 4:04 PM EDT October 30, 2017, https://www.fox61.com/article/entertainment/arts/cas-artist/house-of-cards-ending-amid-kevin-spacey-sexual-harassment-claim/520-22c1e2b8-366d-4a44-bbd9-644176124344

5. Anna Giaritelli, Washington Examiner, California clears first hurdle to breaking into three states, 7:09 AM EDT October 30, 2017, https://www.foxnews.com/politics/california-clears-first-hurdle-to-breaking-into-three-states

6. Caleb Parke, Antifa apocalypse? Anarchist group's plan to overthrow Trump 'regime' starts Saturday, Published November 3, 2017 5:44pm EDT; foxnews.com

Chapter 2

7. David Krayden, Daily Caller, Pull Your Children Out: Candace Owens Says Public Schools Are Brainwashing Children To Embrace 'Marxist Principles', 10 October 2021; https://dailycaller.com/2021/10/10/candace-owens-public-schools-children-maria-bartiromo/

8. Monisha Ravisetti., CNET News, Ancient Mars lake could be hiding fossilized signs of alien life, 8 October 2021, https://www.cnet.com/science/ancient-lake-on-mars-could-be-hiding-fossilized-signs-of-alien-life/

9. Hollie Beale, Express, Jane Fonda, 83, shares what she thinks happens when you die… and it's truly uplifting, 10:08, Wed, Sep 29, 2021 | UPDATED: 10:34, Wed, Sep 29, 2021; https://www.express.co.uk/celebrity-news/1497794/Jane-Fonda-what-happens-when-you-die-uplifting-age-young-grace-and-frankie-news-latest

10. Laura M. Holson, The New York Times, Are We Living in a Post-Happiness World? Sept. 28, 2019; https://www.nytimes.com/2019/09/28/sunday-review/joy-happiness-life.html

Chapter 3

11. Valerie Richardson, Washington Times, Pfizer scientist admits that natural antibodies are probably better than vaccination, millions are naturally immune, 5 October 2021,

https://www.washingtontimes.com/news/2021/oct/5/project-veritas-captures-pfizer-scientists-giving-/

12. The Associated Press, Tragic milestone as Covid-19 deaths eclipse 700,000 in U.S., Oct. 2, 2021, 10:31 AM EDT / Updated Oct. 2, 2021, 3:55 PM EDT, https://apnews.com/article/coronavirus-pandemic-health-pandemics-public-health-80209c66802902e42adfbe075ff5272b

13. Angela Dewan, CNN, Greta Thunberg roasts world leaders for being 'blah, blah, blah on climate action, 28 September 2021, updated 29 September 2021, https://www.cnn.com/2021/09/28/world/greta-thunberg-climate-intl/index.html

14. Stephanie Ebbs, ABC News, EPA plans to roll back Clean Power Plan, major Obama-era climate rule, October 9, 2017, https://abcnews.go.com/Politics/epa-plans-repeal-clean-power-plan-major-obama/story?id=50370078

15. Kenneth Chang, New York Times and Science News, Hubble Space Telescope Spots Earliest and Farthest Star Known, Characterizing the earliest galaxies in the universe, only 200 million years after the Big Bang" Published March 30, 2022, Updated April 1, 2022, https://www.nytimes.com/2022/03/30/science/hubble-star-big-bang.html

16. Tara Law, Time Magazine, Surgeon General Adams Warns of 'Saddest Week of Most Americans' Lives' as COVID-19 Pandemic Spreads, updated: April 6, 2020 9:29am EDT, Originally Published: April

5, 2020 2:31pm EDT, https://time.com/5815870/
jerome-adams-surgeon-general-saddest-week-covid-19/

Chapter 4

17. Mark Lungariello, New York Post Missouri Executes
    Ernest Johnson for 1994 triple murder, October
    5, 2021, 8:53pm, https://nypost.com/2021/10/05/
    missouri-executes-ernest-johnson-for-1994-triple-murder/

18. Jerry L., Sadistic Monster with No Heart; Texas Man Gets Two
    Life Sentences For Crashing Propane Tank-Filled Truck into
    RV with Pregnant Ex Inside, 4 Oct 2021, Law& Crime; https://
    lawandcrime.com/crime/a-sadistic-monster-with-no-heart-
    texas-man-gets-two-life-sentences-for-crashing-propane-
    tank-filled-truck-into-rv-with-pregnant-ex-inside/

19. Kaitlin Sullivan, Inverse, What is the limit to human life? A
    striking number explained, here's why more people will live
    beyond 100 in the future, SEP. 30, 2021, https://www.inverse.
    com/mind-body/maximum-human-age-longevity-science

20. Crime and Justice News, Biden Administration Drops 7 Death
    Penalty Requests," Arizona State University, July 22, 2021,
    https://www.nytimes.com/2021/07/22/nyregion/justice-de-
    partment-death-penalty.html

21. Matt Leach, Fox News, DC Mayor bans dancing
    at weddings; it's insane, Published May 3, 2021
    1:13pm EDT, https://www.foxnews.com/lifestyle/
    bride-sues-mayor-dancing-ban-weddings

22. AP News, Jury recommends death in Oklahoma beheading case; Associated Press October 12, 2017, https://apnews.com/ b68d6d4bc45043b6a1b94b1e9150061e/Oklahoma-jury-recommends-the-death-penalty-in-beheading-case

23. Michael L., Fox News, Sienna confronted by immigration activists in bathroom, 2 Oct 2021, https://www.foxnews.com/politics/ sinema-confronted-by-immigration-activists-in-a-bathroom

24. Tal Kopan, Maeve Reston, CNN, The Deferred Action for Childhood Arrivals (DACA); what's the problem? "Historic immigration debate to grip Senate, February 12, 2018, July 18, 2021 https://www.cnn.com/2021/07/18/politics/ daca-ruling-young-undocumented-immigrants-frustration/ index.html

25. Edmund DeMarche, Fox News, Judge rules against Trump administration on rescinding DACA, January 9, 2018, Published January 10, 2018 11:37am EST, https://www.fox-news.com/politics/judge-rules-against-trump-administra-tion-on-rescinding-daca

26. Kim Painter, USA TODAY, Deaths and hospitalizations rise as flu season hits full swing, Jan. 10, 2018, https://www.usatoday. com/story/news/2018/01/09/deaths-and-hospitalizations-rise-flu-season-hits-full-swing/1017898001/

27. Ryan Struyk, CNN, CNN poll: Most Americans oppose Trump's tax reform plan, updated October 19, 2017, https:// www.cnn.com/2017/10/18/politics/poll-trump-tax-reform/ index.html

28. Kaitlyn Schallhorn, Fox News, Trump's tax reform plan: Who are the winners and losers? Published October 26, 2017 10:25am EDT, https://www.foxnews.com/politics/trumps-tax-reform-plan-who-are-the-winners-and-losers

Chapter 5

29. Sebastian K. Express, End of the world: Scientists send dire ocean tide warning as Moon is slowly 'leaving us' , 4 October 2021, https://www.express.co.uk/news/science/1500740/end-of-the-world-ocean-tide-weather-warning-moon-leave-earth-gravity-orbit

30. Kaelan D. Washington Examiner, Romanian billionaire and family dead after crashing plane in Milan, October 04, 2021 01:32 PM, https://www.washingtonexaminer.com/news/romanian-billionaire-and-family-among-eight-dead-in-plane

31. Christopher R., AP Economics Writer, Treasury Secretary Janet Yellen warns delay in raising debt limit will slow economy, 28 September 2021, https://apnews.com/article/business-united-states-bills-economy-janet-yel-len-de159a96c61d0679e06bde313881092c

32. Fox News, According to Christian numerologist David Meade the world will end on 23 Sept 2017. Published September 15, 2017, https://www.foxnews.com/science/biblical-prophecy-claims-the-world-will-end-on-sept-23-christian-numerolo-gists-claim

Chapter 6

33. Chip Chick, She Was 12-Years-Old and 9 Months Pregnant When She Disappeared Into The Cold December Night 25 Years Ago, 10 October 2021, True Crime, https://www.chipchick.com/2021/10/she-was-12-years-old-and-9-months-pregnant-when-she-disappeared-into-the-cold-december-night.html

34. IE Staff, Inside Edition, A Colorado Woman Who Refused COVID-19 Vaccine Because of Her Faith Is Denied Kidney Transplant., First Published: 12:31 PM PDT, October 8, 2021, https://www.insideedition.com/a-colorado-woman-who-refused-covid-19-vaccine-because-of-her-faith-is-denied-kidney-transplant

35. Hannah W., The Sacramento Bee, Removing a condom without consent is now a violation of California's civil code under new law, 8 October 2021, https://www.reuters.com/world/us/california-law-prohibits-secretly-removing-condom-during-sex-2021-10-08/

36. Hope Cambell, The List, How Clint Eastwood Really Feels about Religion, Clint Eastwood Is Not A Fan Of Organized Religion, OCT. 13, 2021 1:51 PM EST, https://www.thelist.com/631926/how-clint-eastwood-really-feels-about-religion/

37. Peter McIndoe, New Statesman, Birds aren't real and this man wants the world to know, 13 October 2021, https://www.newstatesman.com/culture/2021/10/birds-arent-real-and-this-man-wants-the-world-to-know

38. Martin Burger, Life Site News, CNN's 'Catholic' Chris Cuomo: Americans don't need help from above. The self-professed Catholic and supporter of abortion said God's help is not needed for things to get better in this country. Jul 6, 2020, https://catholicanada.com/2020/07/cnns-catholic-chris-cuomo-americans-dont-need-help-from-above/

Chapter 7

39. Bill Galluccio, National News, Woman Accused Of Using $4.9 Million Police Settlement To Buy Guns For Gang, 9 Oct 2021, https://www.iheart.com/content/2021-10-09-woman-accused-of-using-49-million-police-settlement-to-buy-guns-for-gang/

40. Matthew Michelone, WTAJ News, Out of the Darkness Walk 2017; Posted: Sep. 14, 2017, 04:00 PM EDT, https://www.wtaj.com/centralpalive/out-of-the-darkness-walk-2017/

41. Murugi Thande, Stephanie Ramirez, WUAS9 News, 22-year-old woman killed after 12-year-old boy jumps from overpass in suicide attempt, Published: 11:23 PM EDT October 30, 2017, Updated: 11:23 PM EDT October 30, 2017, https://www.firstcoastnews.com/article/news/22-year-old-woman-killed-after-12-year-old-boy-jumps-from-overpass-in-suicide-attempt/77-487151591

42. World Health Organization, on average, there are 121 suicides per day in the USA alone; even more alarming is that, "On average, one person dies by suicide every 40 seconds somewhere in the world, 9 September 2019, https://www.who.int/news/item/17-06-2021-one-in-100-deaths-is-by-suicide

Chapter 8

43. Kana R, Megachurch With Ferrari-Driving Pastor Gives Back $4.4M Pandemic Loan. , 9 October 2021, Daily Beast, https://news.yahoo.com/megachurch-ferrari-driving-pastor-re-pays-205357541.html

44. Nick Givas, Fox News, Homelessness in Los Angeles County and Homeless encampments increasingly affecting California train traffic; 14 February, 2020, https://www.foxnews.com/us/homelessness-in-los-angeles-here-are-the-statistics

45. Ami Lieu, Fox News, Facing backlash, California County rescinds homeless shelter plan. March 28, 2018, https://www.foxnews.com/politics/facing-backlash-california-county-re-scinds-homeless-shelter-plan

46. Tori Richards, Fox News, 'National disgrace': Community fights back as California overrun by homelessness, human waste, needles. Published February 26, 2018 12:17pm EST, https://www.foxnews.com/politics/national-disgrace-commu-nity-fights-back-as-california-overrun-by-homelessness-hu-man-waste-needles

47. Jeremy Harlan, CNN, Tiny homes for homeless veterans; CNN February 13, 2018, https://www.cnn.com/2018/02/13/us/tiny-houses-homeless-veterans-kansas-city/index.html

Chapter 9

48. Suzanne Sng, The Straights Time, Blackpink's Lisa breaks two Guinness records with solo debut Lalisa, 9 October 2021, PUBLISHED OCT 10, 2021 AT 5:35 AM SGT, https://www.

straitstimes.com/life/entertainment/blackpinks-lisa-breaks-two-guinness-records-with-solo-debut-lalisa

49. Toyin Owoseje, CNN, Nicole Thea, 24-year-old YouTube star, dies along with unborn child. Thea had amassed more than 80,000 subscribers on her YouTube channel, where she often discussed her pregnancy journey and posted content featuring boyfriend Global Boga — real name Jeffery Frimpong — who is a street dancer, Jul 13 2020, https://www.cnn.com/2020/07/13/entertainment/nicole-thea-dies-pregnant-youtuber-intl-scli-gbr/index.html

Chapter 10

50. Verve Times, Paul McCartney wrote a play with John Lennon about JESUS and he just found the manuscript, George S., Speaking with Evening Standard in March 1966, John said: Christianity will go. It will vanish and shrink ... We're more popular than Jesus now–I don't know which will go first, rock and roll or Christianity" 11 October 2021, https://www.express.co.uk/entertainment/music/1504058/Paul-McCartney-Jesus-play-John-Lennon-The-Beatles

Chapter 11

51. Valerie Tarico, Rawstory, These 15 Bible texts reveal why 'God's Own Party' keeps demeaning women, 11 October 2021, https://www.rawstory.com/gop-women/

52. Jonathan Petersen, Bible Gateway Blog, A Catholic reads the Bible. CNN, August 31, 2015, https://www.biblegateway.com/blog/2015/08/cnn-a-catholic-reads-the-bible/

Chapter 12

53. Cameron Frew, UNILAD, Lottery winner dies with winning ticket still in his pocket, Published 18:36, 29 September 2021 BST, https://www.unilad.com/news/lottery-winner-dies-with-winning-ticket-still-in-his-pocket/

54. IE Staff, California Man Wins Lottery 4 times in 6 Months for More Than $6 Million, Nearly 70% of lottery winners end up broke within seven years. Even worse, several winners have died tragically or witnessed those close to them suffer. Inside Edition, Updated: 8:14 AM PDT, May 20, 2018, First Published: 8:13 AM PDT, May 20, 2018, https://news.yahoo.com/man-wins-lottery-4-times-151340069.html

Chapter 13

55. Stephanie Coontz, CNN, How unmarried Americans are changing everything. Why aren't Millennials getting married? Updated 9:13 PM ET, Thu September 21, 2017, https://www.cnn.com/2017/09/21/opinions/how-unmarried-americans-are-changing-the-game-coontz/index.html

56. Mary Papenfuss, HUFFPOST, North Carolina Lt. Gov. Refuses to Resign After Calling LGBTQ Community 'Filth', Oct 8, 2021, 09:43 PM EDT, https://www.huffpost.com/entry/north-carolina-mark-robinson-lgbtq-filth-resignation_n_6160d57de4b0fc312c974d3a

57. Lisa Respers France, CNN Digital, Dave Chappelle sparks LGBTQ+ controversy again, By Lisa F., CNN, Oct. 6, 2021 2:08 p.m. EDT, https://www.cnn.com/2021/10/06/entertainment/dave-chappelle-netflix-controversy/index.html

58. SARAH TAYLOR, Blaze Media/News, Playboy releases October cover featuring a man dressed in women's lingerie and heels, 4 October 2021, https://www.theblaze.com/news/playboy-october-cover-man-lingerie-heels

59. Ben Westcott and Lucie Morris-Marr, CNN, Australia votes 'yes' to same-sex marriage, CNN November 14, 2017, https://www.cnn.com/2017/11/14/asia/australia-same-sex-marriage-yes/index.html

60. BBC UK, Oklahoma mother will go to jail for marrying her daughter, 15 March 2018, https://www.bbc.co.uk/news/world-us-canada-43418891

61. The York Times, Transgender people will be allowed to enlist in the military as court case advances NY Times, December 11 2017, https://www.nytimes.com/2017/12/11/us/politics/transgender-military-pentagon.html

62. Jay Valle, NBC News, Gay penguins raise newly hatched chick at New York zoo, Feb. 2, 2022, 10:52 AM EST, Updated Feb. 2, 2022, 11:42 AM EST, https://www.nbcnews.com/nbc-out/out-news/gay-penguins-raise-newly-hatched-chick-new-york-zoo-rcna14547

63. AWR Hawkins, Breitbart News, 40 Shot During Weekend in Mayor Lori Lightfoot's Chicago, 4 Oct 2021, https://www.breitbart.com/politics/2021/10/11/nearly-40-shot-during-weekend-in-mayor-lori-lightfoots-chicago/

64. Eric Levenson, CNN, Why does the Las Vegas shooter's motive even matter? The answer, according to experts in profiling mass shooters, is that we dig into the motive of mass

killings to try to prevent future attacks, adjust policy and
— perhaps most of all — satisfy our own human curiosity.
Updated 5:54 PM ET, Sat October 7, 2017, https://edition.cnn.
com/2017/10/07/us/las-vegas-shooting-motive/index.html

65. On Point, NPR Radio SC, Texas church massacre: Timeline
of US church shootings Nov. 05, 2017–2:56–At least 26
people are dead in the Sutherland Springs, Texas church
massacre. Here is a look back at the deadliest church shootings in U.S. history" WHY!!!??? "What is wrong with us;
why are there so many mass shootings in the US?"October
3, 2017 https://www.npr.org/2017/11/05/562236373/
what-we-know-from-the-scene-texas-church-shooting

66. The horror of Las Vegas and the hope of heaven. Pastor
Robert Jeffress, Fox News contributor; October 2, 2017,
https://www.foxnews.com/opinion/pastor-robert-jeffress-the-
horror-of-las-vegas-and-the-hope-of-heaven

67. William Mansell, Emily Shapiro and Josh Margolin, ABC
News, ET, 8 killed in mass shooting at Indianapolis FedEx
facility; suspect, 19, was former employee, The 19-year-old
suspect died from an apparent self-inflicted gunshot wound,
April 18, 2021, 11:20 PM, https://abcnews.go.com/US/
multiple-people-shot-indianapolis-fedex-facility-police/
story?id=77109792

68. Associated Press, AT least seven are dead after a gunman
opened fire at a birthday party in a Colorado Springs trailer
park where children were present, The US Sun May 9, 2021,
https://www.theguardian.com/us-news/2021/may/09/
colorado-springs-shooting-birthday-party

Chapter 14

69. Natasha W., Mirror, Teen wrote note begging family 'not to be ashamed' before taking her own life, 9 October 2021, https://www.mirror.co.uk/news/uk-news/teen-wrote-note-begging-family-25177518

70. The Atlanta Journal-Constitution, Do you agree, disagree with Donald Trump's comments on NFL player protests? 7:19 p.m. Sunday, Sept. 24, 2017, https://www.ajc.com/sports/football/you-agree-disagree-with-donald-trump-comments-nfl-player-protests/Yr8Jk1U6AuCnl3NPePQ35H/

Chapter 15

71. Brad R. Fulton, Indiana University, Americans are in a mental health crisis — especially African-Americans. Can churches help? Brad R. F., 8 October 2021, https://theconversation.com/americans-are-in-a-mental-health-crisis-especially-african-americans-can-churches-help-167871

72. Pew Research, In U.S., Decline of Christianity Continues at Rapid Pace, An update on America's changing religious landscape Pew research center–October 17, 2019, https://www.pewresearch.org/religion/2019/10/17/in-u-s-decline-of-christianity-continues-at-rapid-pace/

Chapter 16

73. Houston Kenne, Fox News, Michigan redistricting committee rejects Pledge of Allegiance at meetings: 'To

divisive'–April 2021, https://www.foxnews.com/politics/
michigan-committee-pledge-of-allegiance-divisive

74. Karu F. D., New York Daily News, After family members contracted COVID-19, Ozzy Osbourne says worshiping Satan
protected him from virus, 12 October 2021, https://www.
nydailynews.com/snyde/ny-ozzy-osbourne-credits-devil-wor-
ship-for-protection-against-covid19-pandemic-20211011-
7ewnchrkebhnxhd6zs5sxvcyne-story.html

Chapter 17

75. The Onion, Questions To Ask Yourself Before Starting An
Open Relationship. The Orion (Humor), 9 October 5, 2021,
https://www.theonion.com/questions-to-ask-yourself-before-
starting-an-open-relat-1847785705

76. MIND MATTERS- NEWS, James Webb Telescope show
Big Bang didn't happen? Wait… The unexpected new data
coming back from the telescope are inspiring panic among
astronomers, AUGUST 13, 2022, updated December 31, 2022,
https://mindmatters.ai/2022/08/james-webb-space-telescope-
shows-big-bang-didnt-happen-wait/

Chapter 18

77. Khadean Coombs, CNN, Sporting legend Michael Jordan
donated $10 million to open health clinics in his home-
town of Wilmington, North Carolina." Feb 15, 2021, https://
www.cnn.com/2021/02/15/us/michael-jordan-clinics-dona-
tion-trnd/index.html

78. Will Carless and Alain Stephens, The Trace, Black People Formed One of the Largest Militias in the U.S. Now Its Leader Is In Prosecutors Crosshairs, Oct 8, 2021 Updated Oct 21, 2021, https://www.thetrace.org/2021/10/nfac-black-militia-grandmaster-jay-prosecution/

79. Virginia Kruta, The Daily Caller, Joy Behar Says Black People Shouldn't Be Scared Of COVID Vaccine Anymore Because White People Were The 'Experiment, 7 October 2021, https://dailycaller.com/2021/10/07/the-view-whoopi-joy-behar-black-people-scared-vaccines-covid-19-white-people-tails-experiment/

80. Houston Kenne, Fox News, Schools across America launch BLM 'week of action' featuring four controversial national demands", 2 Feb 2022, https://www.foxnews.com/politics/schools-across-america-blm-week-action-nuclear-family

81. CNN News, Brian Flores tells CNN his kids were inspiration to file lawsuit against NFL and 3 teams alleging racial discrimination, 2 Feb 2022, https://whdh.com/sports/brian-flores-tells-cnn-his-kids-were-inspiration-to-file-lawsuit-against-nfl-and-3-teams-alleging-racial-discrimination/

82. JANAKI CHADHA, Politico, New York City mayor apologizes for calling white cops 'crackers', 02/04/2022 04:37 PM EST, https://www.politico.com/news/2022/02/04/new-york-city-mayor-apologizes-for-calling-white-cops-crackers-00005887

Chapter 19

83. COLIN KALMBACHER, Law & Crime, I Took Your V Card and You Liked It : Kentucky Woman Allegedly Raped 12-Year-Old Boy, Made Him and His Friends Call Her 'Mom, OCT 5, 2021 12:48 PM, https://lawandcrime.com/crime/i-took-your-v-card-and-you-liked-it-kentucky-woman-allegedly-raped-12-year-old-boy-made-him-and-his-friends-call-her-mom/

84. Megan Trimble, National News, STD cases hit record high in US, The CDC reports that cases of sexually transmitted diseases such as chlamydia, gonorrhea, and syphilis reached an all-time high in 2016. But who or what is to blame for the rising STD numbers? September 27, 2017, https://www.usnews.com/news/national-news/articles/2017-09-27/cdc-new-std-cases-hit-record-high-in-the-us

Chapter 20

85. Cedric Thornton, BLACK ENTERPRISE, Black High School Quarterback Ejected after Complaining to Ref About Opponent Calling Him a Racial Slur, 5 October 2021, https://www.blackenterprise.com/black-high-school-quarterback-ejected-after-complaining-to-ref-about-opponent-calling-him-a-racial-slur/

86. Justin Vallejo, INDEPENDENT, Black woman accused of posing as white Ku Klux Klan member to threaten neighbors faces terrorist charges, 5 Oct 2021, https://www.independent.co.uk/news/world/americas/crime/black-woman-kkk-threatens-neighbours-b1932222.html

87. YOUTUBE, Sen. Coleman Young II Speaks out against racial injustice–9-27-2017, https://www.youtube.com > watch?v=AXT3Km4cRNQ

Chapter 21

88. John Blake, CNN, The Black church is having a moment, February 16, 2021, https://www.cnn.com/2021/02/16/us/black-church-pew-pbs-moment/index.html

Chapter 22

89. Tim O'Donnell, Yahoo News, Biden ally suggests Iowa caucus process more restrictive than Texas voting law, 9 October 2021, https://news.yahoo.com/biden-ally-suggests-iowa-caucus-160842482.html

90. Jim Acosta, Jeff Zeleny, Elizabeth Landers, Kaitlan Collins and Kevin Liptak, CNN, Trump infuriated after backing Alabama loser, Updated 10:23 AM ET, Wed September 27, 2017, https://www.cnn.com/2017/09/27/politics/donald-trump-alabama-race-roy-moore/index.html

91. Stephen Collinson and Maeve Reston, CNN, CNN, Biden defeats Trump in an election he made about character of the nation and the President, November 7, 2020, https://www.cnn.com/2020/11/07/politics/joe-biden-wins-us-presidential-election/index.html

Chapter 23

92. Mike G., Epoch Times, The Marxist Underpinnings of BLM Organizations, 9 October 2021, https://www.podchaser.

com/podcasts/american-thought-leaders-887867/episodes/
mike-gonzalez-the-marxist-unde-99739341

93. Daniella Silva, NBC News, Weathering the One day at a time: Bahamians displaced by Dorian seek solace in South Florida, Sep. 12, 2019, 3:37 PM EDT, https://www.nbcnews.com/news/weather/dorian

94. Fox News, Russia launches full-scale attack in Ukraine, dozens dead: 23 Feb 2022, https://www.foxnews.com/world/russian-invades-ukraine-largest-europe-attack-wwii

95. Maegan Vazquez, Kevin Liptak, Betsy Klein and Sam Fossum, CNN, Biden says he's now convinced Putin has decided to invade Ukraine, but leaves door open for diplomacy, February 19, 2022, https://edition.cnn.com/2022/02/18/politics/joe-biden-russia-ukraine/index.html?ref=en.thebell.io

Chapter 24

96. Foreign Policy; The Trump Doctrine: Terrorists Lose and Peace Wins, WH- October 30, 2020, https://trumpwhitehouse.archives.gov/articles/terrorists-are-losing-and-peace-is-breaking-out/

97. Washington Post, Trump's racism and xeno-phobia haven't caught on, Sept 13, 2020, https://www.washingtonpost.com/opinions/2020/09/13/trump-racism-xenophobia-havent-caught/

Chapter 25

98. New York Times, Alcohol Abuse Is on the Rise, but Doctors Too Often Fail to Treat it, 12 July 2021, https://www.ncbi.nlm. nih.gov/search/research-news/14056/

99. CATHERINE T., ESPN President John Skipper resigns citing substance abuse issue, December 18, 2017; Parents mourn son's 'senseless' and 'horrific' death following alleged hazing incident at LSU fraternity By Dec 14, 2017, https://abcnews.go.com/US/espn-president-john-skipper-resigns-citing-substance-abuse/story?id=51861290

100. ASSOCIATED PRESS, Autopsy: Oklahoma State student died of alcohol poisoning — Associated Press, January 17, 2017, AT 2:38PM, https://apnews.com/article/bf18ce2af9c54f4fb81cad26a0b62018

101. Baltimore City Health Department, Deaths from drug, alcohol overdoses skyrocket in Maryland (Baltimore Sun) Friday Jun 9th, 2017, https://health. maryland.gov/vsa/Documents/Overdose/Quarterly Drug_Alcohol_Intoxication_Report_2021_Q3.pdf

Chapter 26

102. JOSEF FEDERMAN, AP News, Israeli court ruling on major holy site angers Palestinians, 7 October 2021, https:// apnews.com/article/jerusalem-israel-middle-east-religion-islam-fc56fed1ebb935912e863353f327c184

103. Aljazeera, Israel's election ended with neither a Netanyahu-led bloc nor an alliance of his opponents winning a majority, 6 Apr 2021, https://www.aljazeera.com/news/2021/4/6/israels-president-to-announce-candidate-to-form-new-government

CPSIA information can be obtained
at www.ICGtesting.com
Printed in the USA
LVHW071918090523
746536LV00014B/200